Mmmm...
One Pot

Mmmm...
One Pot

This edition published in 2011

LOVE FOOD is an imprint of Parragon Books Ltd

Parragon
Queen Street House
4 Queen Street
Bath BA1 1HE, UK

ISBN: 978-1-4454-2786-7

Printed in China

Design by Talking Design
Cover photography by Charlie Richards
Cover image styled by Mary Wall
Introduction by Linda Doeser

Notes for the Reader
This book uses both metric and imperial measurements. Follow the same units of measurement throughout; do not mix metric and imperial. All spoon measurements are level: teaspoons are assumed to be 5 ml, and tablespoons are assumed to be 15 ml. Unless otherwise stated, milk is assumed to be full fat, eggs and individual vegetables are medium, and pepper is freshly ground black pepper.

The times given are an approximate guide only. Preparation times differ according to the techniques used by different people and the cooking times may also vary from those given. Optional ingredients, variations or serving suggestions have not been included in the calculations.

Recipes using raw or very lightly cooked eggs should be avoided by infants, the elderly, pregnant women, convalescents and anyone suffering from an illness. Pregnant and breastfeeding women are advised to avoid eating peanuts and peanut products. Sufferers from nut allergies should be aware that some of the ready-made ingredients used in the recipes in this book may contain nuts. Always check the packaging before use.

contents

introduction

There is nothing more comforting than a home-cooked one-pot dish, whether tender beef and mushrooms immersed in a rich red wine sauce or a filling mixture of spicy vegetables and dried beans. While we tend to think of one-pot dishes as cold-weather food, there are also many lighter dishes that are ideal for warmer times of year. What could be more delicious on a summer's evening than an aromatic fish and seafood stew eaten alfresco or a colourful medley of Mediterranean vegetables served with fresh crusty bread?

The term casserole was originally applied just to the cooking vessel that we all recognize – an ovenproof pot with a lid – but soon came to refer to any dish that is cooked in it as well. Casseroling is a method of cooking that is slow and unhurried, allowing plenty of time for tougher cuts of meat and vegetables to become tender and for the cooking juices to thicken and acquire a rich flavour. However, the same could be said of stewing. The latter might involve using a little more liquid, although not invariably, and is traditionally cooked on the hob rather than in the oven.

There are many international versions of the casserole with their variations in technique, as well as ingredients. A French daube is a slowly braised dish that was once cooked in a tall casserole with a special lid that could be filled with hot charcoal. When suspended over the fire, it benefited from heat from below and above. A Moroccan tagine is a shallow round earthenware dish with a conical lid that traps steam and so ensures that the ingredients are kept moist throughout the long cooking time over a small, round charcoal brazier. Like casserole, the word tagine is now applied to the dish as well as the vessel. Both dishes can be cooked just as successfully in a casserole dish in a modern oven.

Nowadays, the name casserole can be applied to a multitude of different dishes, but it is usually a one-pot dish with a mixture of ingredients – meat, poultry, fish, vegetables, and even rice or pasta – that is often served in the vessel in which it is cooked. It could be cooked in the traditional casserole dish, either on the hob or in the oven, in a saucepan or even in a baking dish. It might be called a casserole, stew, ragoût, bake, cobbler, hot pot, cassoulet, carbonade or mole…the list goes on. Whatever it contains and however it's cooked, there is no denying that the casserole is a truly delicious dish!

top tips for success

- A flameproof, ovenproof casserole dish can be used to brown meat or other ingredients over a direct heat on the hob before being transferred to the oven to finish cooking. Make sure to choose one with a tight-fitting lid to prevent moisture from being lost during cooking.

- When cutting up meat for a casserole, try to make the pieces the same size to ensure even cooking. If some are much smaller than others, they may overcook and become stringy. Always remove and discard any gristle and trim off excess fat. Unless you're being particularly health conscious, you do not need to remove all marbled fat as it will add richness and flavour to the cooking juices. If you are worried about fat, the easiest way to ensure that almost all of it is removed is to prepare the casserole the day before it is required, chill it in the refrigerator and then lift off any fat solidified on the surface before reheating.

- Meat is almost always browned first in order to seal in the juices and give it an attractive brown colour. It may be coated in flour, which helps to thicken the cooking juices. Add the pieces of meat to the hot pan in small batches. Turn them over as soon as they are browned on one side and remove with a slotted spoon when they are sealed all over.

- An easy way to coat pieces of meat with flour is to put them into a polythene bag, add the seasoned flour, hold the bag closed and shake well. Shake off any excess flour from the meat before cooking.

- If the sediment in the base of the pan looks as if it might scorch, stir in a little of the recipe's liquid – water, wine, stock, beer or cider – between sealing batches of meat. Taste and if it isn't burnt, set aside to add with the main quantity of liquid later.

- Onions and sometimes other vegetables need to be softened before they are combined with the other ingredients. This is usually best done separately from browning the meat.

- Cooking times in the recipes are always guidelines rather than hard-and-fast rules and you cannot speed up the cooking without catastrophic results. Try to build a little 'slack' into your schedule so that if your particular batch of meat or pulses is not quite tender at the recommended time, the family won't faint from hunger when the casserole requires a further 15–30 minutes in the oven. Do not increase the oven temperature in the vain hope that cooking will speed up.

- Check the quantity of liquid in the casserole from time to time during cooking. If it seems to be drying out, stir in a little hot stock or water. If the juices still seem to be a little too runny towards the end of the cooking time, remove the lid to allow the excess liquid to evaporate and the juices to thicken.

- For a fresh bouquet garni, tie 1 fresh thyme sprig, 2 fresh flat-leaf parsley sprigs and 1 fresh bay leaf together with kitchen string. Use a long piece of string and tie to the handle of the casserole or pan so that the bouquet garni dangles into the hot liquid but is easy to remove. Do not forget to remove and discard the bouquet garni, or any other whole herbs or spices, such as bay leaves, star anise and cinnamon.

béchamel sauce

makes about 600 ml/1 pint
- 600 ml/1 pint milk
- 1 bay leaf
- 6 black peppercorns
- slice of onion
- blade of mace
- 50 g/1¾ oz butter
- 50 g/1¾ oz plain flour
- salt and pepper

1 Pour the milk into a saucepan and add the bay leaf, peppercorns, onion and mace.

2 Heat gently to just below boiling point, then remove from the heat, cover and leave to infuse for 10 minutes.

3 Strain the milk into a jug. Melt the butter in a separate saucepan. Sprinkle in the flour and cook over a low heat, stirring constantly, for 1 minute.

4 Remove from the heat and gradually stir in the warm milk. Return to the heat and bring to the boil, then cook, stirring, until thickened and smooth. Season to taste with salt and pepper and set aside.

beef stock

makes about 1.7 litres/3 pints
- 1 kg/2 lb 4 oz beef marrow bones, cut into 7.5-cm/3-inch pieces
- 650 g/1 lb 7 oz stewing steak in a single piece
- 2.8 litres/5 pints water
- 4 cloves
- 2 onions, halved
- 2 celery sticks, roughly chopped
- 8 black peppercorns
- 1 bouquet garni

1 Place the bones in a large saucepan and put the meat on top. Add the water and gradually bring to the boil, skimming off the foam that rises to the surface.

2 Press a clove into each onion half and add to the pan with the celery, peppercorns and bouquet garni. Partially cover and simmer for 3 hours. Remove the meat and simmer for a further hour.

3 Strain the stock into a bowl, leave to cool, cover and store in the refrigerator. When cold, remove and discard the layer of fat from the surface. Use immediately or freeze for up to 6 months.

chicken stock

makes about 2.5 litres/4½ pints
- 1.3 kg/3 lb chicken wings and necks
- 2 onions, cut into wedges
- 4 litres/7 pints water
- 2 carrots, roughly chopped
- 2 celery sticks, roughly chopped
- 10 fresh parsley sprigs
- 4 fresh thyme sprigs
- 2 bay leaves
- 10 black peppercorns

1 Place the chicken wings and necks and the onions in a large saucepan and cook over a low heat, stirring frequently, until lightly browned.

2 Add the water and stir well to scrape off any sediment from the base of the pan. Gradually bring to the boil, skimming off the foam that rises to the surface. Add all the remaining ingredients, partially cover and simmer for 3 hours.

3 Strain the stock into a bowl, leave to cool, cover and store in the refrigerator. When cold, remove and discard the layer of fat from the surface. Use immediately or freeze for up to 6 months.

fish stock

makes about 1.3 litres/2¼ pints
- 650 g/1 lb 7 oz white fish heads, bones and trimmings, rinsed
- 1 onion, sliced
- 2 celery sticks, chopped
- 1 carrot, sliced
- 1 bay leaf
- 4 fresh parsley sprigs
- 4 black peppercorns
- ½ lemon, sliced
- 1.3 litres/2¼ pints water
- 125 ml/4 fl oz dry white wine

1 Cut out and discard the gills from the fish heads, then place the heads, bones and trimmings in a saucepan.

2 Add all the remaining ingredients and gradually bring to the boil, skimming off the foam that rises to the surface. Partially cover and simmer for 25 minutes.

3 Strain the stock without pressing down on the contents of the sieve. Leave to cool, cover and store in the refrigerator. Use immediately or freeze for up to 3 months.

vegetable stock

makes about 1.3 litres/2¼ pints
- 2 tbsp sunflower oil
- 115 g/4 oz onion, finely chopped
- 40 g/1½ oz leek, finely chopped
- 115 g/4 oz carrots, finely chopped
- 4 celery sticks, finely chopped
- 85 g/3 oz fennel, finely chopped
- 1 small tomato, finely chopped
- 2.25 litres/4 pints water
- 1 bouquet garni

1 Heat the oil in a large saucepan. Add the onion and leek and cook over a low heat, stirring occasionally, for 5 minutes, until softened.

2 Add the remaining vegetables, cover and cook for 10 minutes. Add the water and bouquet garni, bring to the boil and simmer for 20 minutes.

3 Strain the stock into a bowl, leave to cool, cover and store in the refrigerator. Use immediately or freeze for up to 3 months.

Mmmm... meat

beef in red wine

serves 8

- 4 tbsp plain flour
- 1 kg/2 lb 4 oz lean stewing steak, diced
- 225 g/8 oz lardons or diced streaky bacon
- 4 tbsp olive oil
- 40 g/1½ oz butter
- 16 baby onions or shallots
- 3 garlic cloves, finely chopped
- 225 g/8 oz mushrooms, sliced
- 600 ml/1 pint full-bodied red wine
- 175 ml/6 fl oz beef stock
- bouquet garni
- salt and pepper
- mashed potatoes, to serve
- fresh flat-leaf parsley sprigs, to garnish

1 Preheat the oven to 160°C/325°F/Gas Mark 3.

2 Season the flour with salt and pepper to taste, and toss the beef in it to coat. Shake off any excess.

3 Heat a large flameproof casserole, add the lardons and cook over a medium heat, stirring frequently, for 5 minutes, until golden brown. Remove with a slotted spoon. Heat the oil in the casserole. Add the beef, in batches, and cook, stirring frequently, for 8–10 minutes, until browned all over. Remove with a slotted spoon.

4 Melt the butter in the casserole, then add the onions and garlic and cook, stirring frequently, for 5 minutes, until light golden brown. Add the mushrooms and cook, stirring occasionally, for a further 5 minutes.

5 Return the beef and lardons to the casserole, pour in the wine and stock, add the bouquet garni and bring to the boil. Cover and transfer the casserole to the preheated oven. Cook, stirring 2–3 times, for 1¾–2 hours, until the beef is very tender. Taste and adjust the seasoning, adding salt and pepper if needed. Remove and discard the bouquet garni. Serve immediately with mashed potatoes, garnished with parsley sprigs.

beef stew with herb dumplings

serves 6

- 3 tbsp olive oil
- 2 onions, finely sliced
- 2 garlic cloves, chopped
- 1 kg/2 lb 4 oz stewing steak, trimmed and cut into strips
- 2 tbsp plain flour
- 300 ml/10 fl oz beef stock
- bouquet garni
- 150 ml/5 fl oz red wine
- salt and pepper

herb dumplings

- 115 g/4 oz self-raising flour
- 55 g/2 oz suet or vegetable shortening
- 1 tsp mustard
- 1 tbsp chopped fresh parsley, plus extra to garnish
- 1 tsp chopped fresh sage
- 4 tbsp cold water
- salt and pepper

1 Preheat the oven to 150°C/300°F/Gas Mark 2.

2 Heat 1 tablespoon of the oil in a large flameproof casserole and fry the onions and garlic until soft and brown. Transfer to a plate.

3 Heat the remaining oil in the casserole. Add the beef, in batches, and cook, stirring frequently, for 8–10 minutes, until browned all over.

4 Sprinkle in the flour and stir well. Season well with salt and pepper. Pour in the stock, stirring all the time, then bring to the boil. Return the onions to the casserole with the bouquet garni and wine. Cover and bake in the preheated oven for 2–2½ hours.

5 For the dumplings, place the flour, suet, mustard, parsley and sage in a bowl with salt and pepper to taste. Mix well, then add enough of the water to form a firm but soft dough. Break the dough into 12 pieces and roll them into round dumplings.

6 Remove the casserole from the oven, discard the bouquet garni and add the dumplings, pushing them down under the liquid. Cover, return to the oven and bake for a further 15 minutes, until the dumplings have doubled in size. Garnish with parsley and serve immediately.

beef goulash

serves 8

- 4 tbsp sunflower oil
- 1 kg/2 lb 4 oz stewing steak, trimmed and cut into cubes
- 1 tbsp plain flour
- 1 tbsp paprika, plus extra for sprinkling
- 600 ml/1 pint beef stock
- 55 g/2 oz butter
- 4 onions, chopped
- 2 carrots, diced
- 1½ tsp caraway seeds
- 1 tsp dried thyme
- 2 bay leaves
- 800 g/1 lb 12 oz canned chopped tomatoes
- 2 tbsp tomato purée
- 3 potatoes, diced
- salt and pepper
- soured cream, to serve

1 Preheat the oven to 160°C/325°F/Gas Mark 3.

2 Heat the oil in a large frying pan. Add the beef, in batches, and cook over a medium heat, stirring frequently, for 8–10 minutes, until browned all over. Reduce the heat to low, sprinkle over the flour and paprika and cook, stirring constantly, for 3–4 minutes. Gradually stir in the stock and bring to the boil, stirring constantly. Remove the pan from the heat and pour the mixture into a casserole.

3 Melt the butter in the rinsed-out frying pan. Add the onions and carrots and cook over a low heat, stirring occasionally, for 5 minutes. Add the caraway seeds, thyme, bay leaves, tomatoes and tomato purée, stir well and cook for 5 minutes. Add the potatoes, season to taste with salt and pepper and bring to the boil.

4 Remove the pan from the heat and pour the mixture into the casserole. Stir, cover, transfer to the preheated oven and cook for 1¾–2 hours, until the meat is tender. Remove from the oven, taste and adjust the seasoning, adding salt and pepper if needed. Remove and discard the bay leaves. Serve the goulash immediately, topped with a swirl of soured cream and a sprinkling of paprika.

vietnamese braised beef & carrots

serves 6

- 100 ml/3½ fl oz Thai fish sauce
- 50 g/1¾ oz palm sugar or granulated sugar
- 1 tsp five-spice powder
- 1.8 kg/4 lb beef short ribs or oxtail, or 1.3 kg/3 lb beef shin, cut into 5-cm/2-inch pieces
- 3 lemon grass stalks
- 1 tbsp vegetable oil
- 8 large garlic cloves, crushed
- 6 small–medium shallots, peeled
- 85 g/3 oz fresh ginger, thinly sliced
- 1.2 litres/2 pints coconut water (not coconut milk) or water
- 500–700 ml/18–24 fl oz water
- 6 star anise
- 1 piece cassia bark or cinnamon stick, about 10 cm/4 inches long
- 4 fresh red bird's eye chillies or dried red Chinese (tien sien) chillies
- 4 large carrots, peeled and cut diagonally into 1 cm/½ inch thick pieces
- salt and pepper
- cooked rice, to serve

1 Put the fish sauce and sugar in a large bowl and whisk until the sugar is completely dissolved. Add the five-spice powder and mix well. Add the meat and turn to coat evenly. Transfer the marinade and meat to a polythene bag and seal the bag, then leave to marinate in the refrigerator, flipping the bag over every hour or so, for 6 hours.

2 Meanwhile, discard the bruised leaves and root ends of the lemon grass stalks, then halve and crush 15–20 cm/6–8 inches of the lower stalks.

3 Heat the oil in a large saucepan over a high heat, then add the garlic, shallots and ginger and stir-fry for 5 minutes, or until golden. Add the coconut water, water, lemon grass, star anise, cassia and chillies.

4 Reduce the heat to low–medium and add the meat and marinade with enough water to cover by about 2.5 cm/1 inch. Simmer, partially covered, for 2 hours, then add the carrots. Cook for a further 2–3 hours, or until the meat is tender and falls off the bones. Adjust the seasoning, adding salt and pepper if needed.

5 Skim off any fat from the surface of the casserole. Serve immediately with rice.

spicy beef cobbler

serves 4

- 2 tbsp plain flour
- 900 g/2 lb stewing steak, cut into bite-sized chunks
- 2 tbsp chilli oil or olive oil
- 1 large onion, sliced
- 1 garlic clove, crushed
- 1 small fresh red chilli, deseeded and chopped
- 1 courgette, sliced
- 1 red pepper, deseeded and cut into small chunks
- 150 g/5½ oz mushrooms, sliced
- 1 tbsp tomato purée
- 500 ml/18 fl oz red wine
- 250 ml/9 fl oz beef or vegetable stock
- 1 bay leaf
- salt and pepper

cobbler topping

- 175 g/6 oz self-raising flour, plus extra for dusting
- 2 tsp baking powder
- pinch of cayenne pepper
- pinch of salt
- 40 g/1½ oz butter
- 4–5 tbsp milk

1 Preheat the oven to 160°C/325°F/Gas Mark 3.

2 Put the flour in a bowl and season well with salt and pepper. Add the beef, toss until well coated and reserve any remaining seasoned flour. Heat half the oil in a flameproof casserole. Add the beef and cook, stirring, until browned all over. Remove with a slotted spoon. Heat the remaining oil in the casserole, add the onion and garlic and cook over a medium heat, stirring, for 2 minutes, until softened. Add the chilli, courgette, red pepper and mushrooms and cook, stirring, for a further 3 minutes.

3 Stir in the remaining seasoned flour and the tomato purée, then stir in the wine. Pour in the stock, add the bay leaf, then bring to the boil. Reduce the heat and cook over a low heat, stirring, until thickened. Return the beef to the casserole, cover and bake in the preheated oven for 45 minutes.

4 Meanwhile, to make the cobbler topping, sift the flour, baking powder, cayenne pepper and salt into a mixing bowl. Rub in the butter until the mixture resembles fine breadcrumbs, then stir in enough of the milk to make a smooth dough. Transfer to a lightly floured work surface, knead lightly, then roll out to a thickness of about 1 cm/½ inch. Cut out rounds using a 5-cm/2-inch biscuit cutter.

5 Remove the casserole from the oven and discard the bay leaf. Arrange the dough rounds over the top, then return to the oven for a further 30 minutes, or until the topping is golden brown. Serve immediately.

beef stew with olives

serves 6

- 750 g/1 lb 10 oz beef topside, cut into 2.5-cm/1-inch cubes
- 2 tbsp olive oil
- 800 g/1 lb 12 oz canned chopped tomatoes
- 225 g/8 oz mushrooms, sliced
- strip of finely pared orange rind
- 55 g/2 oz Bayonne ham, cut into strips
- 12 black olives

marinade

- 350 ml/12 fl oz dry white wine
- 2 tbsp brandy
- 1 tbsp white wine vinegar
- 4 shallots, sliced
- 4 carrots, sliced
- 1 garlic clove, finely chopped
- 6 black peppercorns
- 4 fresh thyme sprigs
- 1 fresh rosemary sprig
- 2 fresh parsley sprigs, plus extra to garnish
- 1 bay leaf
- salt

1 Combine the marinade ingredients in a bowl. Add the beef, stirring to coat, then cover with clingfilm and leave in the refrigerator to marinate for 8 hours, or overnight.

2 Preheat the oven to 150°C/300°F/Gas Mark 2.

3 Drain the beef, reserving the marinade, and pat dry on kitchen paper. Heat the oil in a large flameproof casserole. Add the beef, in batches, and cook over a medium heat, stirring, for 3–4 minutes, or until browned.

4 Add the tomatoes, mushrooms and orange rind. Strain the reserved marinade into the casserole. Bring to the boil, cover and bake in the preheated oven for 2½ hours.

5 Remove the casserole from the oven, add the ham and olives and return to the oven for a further 30 minutes, or until the beef is very tender. Discard the orange rind and serve immediately, garnished with parsley sprigs.

beef en daube with mustard mash

serves 2

- 2 tsp vegetable oil
- 225 g/8 oz extra-lean stewing steak, cut into 8 pieces
- 10 small shallots, peeled but left whole
- 1 garlic clove, crushed
- 1 tomato, chopped
- 100 g/3½ oz mushrooms, finely sliced
- 150 ml/5 fl oz red wine
- 100 ml/3½ fl oz chicken stock
- bouquet garni
- 1 tsp cornflour
- salt and pepper

mustard mash

- 2 floury potatoes, peeled and sliced
- 1½–2 tbsp skimmed milk, heated
- 1 tsp Dijon mustard, or to taste

1 Preheat the oven to 180°C/350°F/Gas Mark 4.

2 Heat the oil in a flameproof casserole. Add the meat and shallots and cook over a high heat, stirring, for 4–5 minutes, until the meat is browned on all sides. Add the garlic, tomato, mushrooms, wine, stock and bouquet garni. Bring to a simmer, cover and transfer to the preheated oven to cook for 45–60 minutes, or until everything is tender.

3 Meanwhile, place the potatoes in a saucepan of boiling water and simmer for 20 minutes, or until just tender. Remove from heat, drain well and return to the saucepan. Add the milk and mash well. Stir in the mustard and keep warm.

4 Use a slotted spoon to remove the meat and vegetables from the casserole and transfer to a warmed serving dish. Cook the sauce on the hob over a high heat until reduced by half. Reduce the heat, remove the bouquet garni and adjust the seasoning, adding salt and pepper if needed.

5 Mix the cornflour to a paste with a little cold water. Add to the sauce, stirring well, and bring back to a simmer. Pour the sauce over the meat and vegetables and serve with the mustard mash.

meatball casserole

serves 4
meatballs

- 1 slice of bread, crusts removed, torn into pieces
- 1½ tbsp milk
- 300 g/10½ oz fresh steak mince
- 2 tbsp chopped fresh parsley, plus extra to garnish
- 1 small egg
- salt and pepper

- 2 tbsp olive oil
- 2 onions, chopped
- 2 garlic cloves, finely chopped
- 500 g/1 lb 2 oz carrots, cut into pieces
- 500 g/1 lb 2 oz potatoes, cut into pieces
- 300 ml/10 fl oz beef stock or water
- 1 tbsp sweet paprika
- 500 ml/18 fl oz passata
- salt and pepper

1 For the meatballs, place the bread in a bowl with the milk and leave to soak for 5 minutes. Put the steak, parsley and egg into a separate bowl. Squeeze out the bread and add it to the bowl, then season to taste with salt and pepper. Mix well until thoroughly combined. Shape the mixture into 16 small balls. Place on a plate, cover and chill in the refrigerator for 30 minutes.

2 Heat the oil in a large saucepan. Add the meatballs, in batches if necessary, and cook over a medium heat, stirring and turning frequently, until browned all over. Remove from the pan and set aside.

3 Add the onions and garlic to the pan and cook over a low heat, stirring occasionally, for 5 minutes. Add the carrots and potatoes, then pour in the stock and bring to the boil. Reduce the heat, cover and simmer for 15 minutes.

4 Add the paprika, stir in the passata and return the meatballs to the pan. Re-cover the pan and simmer for a further 15–20 minutes. Season to taste with salt and pepper, garnish with parsley and serve immediately.

pepper pot stew

serves 4

- 450 g/1 lb stewing steak
- 1½ tbsp plain flour
- 2 tbsp olive oil
- 1 onion, chopped
- 3–4 garlic cloves, crushed
- 1 fresh green chilli, deseeded and chopped
- 3 celery sticks, sliced
- 4 whole cloves
- 1 tsp ground allspice
- 1–2 tsp hot pepper sauce, or to taste
- 600 ml/1 pint beef stock
- 225 g/8 oz squash, such as acorn, deseeded, peeled and cut into small chunks
- 1 large red pepper, deseeded and chopped
- 4 tomatoes, roughly chopped
- 115 g/4 oz okra, trimmed and halved
- cooked rice, to serve

1 Trim any fat or gristle from the beef and cut into 2.5-cm/1-inch chunks. Toss the beef in the flour until well coated and reserve any remaining flour.

2 Heat the oil in a large heavy-based saucepan and cook the onion, garlic, chilli and celery with the cloves and allspice, stirring frequently, for 5 minutes, or until softened. Add the beef and cook over a high heat, stirring frequently, for 3 minutes, or until browned on all sides. Sprinkle in the reserved flour and cook, stirring constantly, for 2 minutes, then remove from the heat.

3 Add the hot pepper sauce and gradually stir in the stock, then return to the heat and bring to the boil, stirring. Reduce the heat, cover and simmer, stirring occasionally, for 1½ hours.

4 Add the squash and red pepper to the saucepan and simmer for a further 15 minutes. Add the tomatoes and okra and simmer for a further 15 minutes, or until the beef is tender. Serve immediately with rice.

beef enchiladas

serves 4
taco sauce

- 1 tbsp olive oil
- 1 onion, finely chopped
- 1 green pepper, deseeded and diced
- 1–2 fresh green chillies, deseeded and finely chopped
- 3 garlic cloves, crushed
- 1 tsp ground cumin
- 1 tsp ground coriander
- 1 tsp soft light brown sugar
- 450 g/1 lb ripe tomatoes, peeled and roughly chopped
- juice of ½ lemon
- salt and pepper

- 2 tbsp olive oil, plus extra for brushing
- 2 large onions, thinly sliced
- 550 g/1 lb 4 oz lean beef, cut into bite-sized pieces
- 1 tbsp ground cumin
- 1–2 tsp cayenne pepper, or to taste
- 1 tsp paprika
- 8 soft corn tortillas, warmed
- 225 g/8 oz Cheddar cheese, grated
- salt and pepper

1 Preheat the oven to 180°C/350°F/Gas Mark 4. Brush a large baking dish with oil.

2 To make the sauce, heat the oil in a frying pan over a medium heat. Add the onion and cook for 5 minutes, or until softened. Stir in the green pepper and chilli and cook for 5 minutes. Add the garlic, cumin, coriander and sugar and cook for a further 2 minutes, stirring. Stir in the tomatoes and lemon juice with salt and pepper to taste. Bring to the boil, then reduce the heat and simmer for 15 minutes.

3 Heat the oil in a large frying pan over a low heat. Add the onions and cook for 10 minutes, or until soft and golden. Remove and set aside.

4 Increase the heat to high, add the beef and cook, stirring, for 2–3 minutes, or until browned on all sides. Reduce the heat to medium, add the spices and salt and pepper to taste, and cook, stirring constantly, for 2 minutes.

5 Divide the beef mixture among the tortillas, top with three quarters of the cheese and roll up. Place the tortillas, seam-side down, in the prepared dish, top with the taco sauce and the remaining cheese and bake in the preheated oven for 30 minutes, until the topping is golden and bubbling. Serve immediately.

lasagne al forno

serves 4
- 2 tbsp olive oil
- 55 g/2 oz pancetta, chopped
- 1 onion, chopped
- 1 garlic clove, finely chopped
- 225 g/8 oz fresh beef mince
- 2 celery sticks, chopped
- 2 carrots, chopped
- pinch of sugar
- ½ tsp dried oregano
- 400 g/14 oz canned chopped tomatoes
- 2 tsp Dijon mustard
- 140 g/5 oz Cheddar cheese, grated
- 300 ml/10 fl oz béchamel sauce (see page 9)
- 225 g/8 oz dried no pre-cook lasagne sheets
- 115 g/4 oz freshly grated Parmesan cheese
- salt and pepper

1 Preheat the oven to 190°C/375°F/Gas Mark 5.

2 Heat the oil in a large heavy-based saucepan. Add the pancetta and cook over a medium heat, stirring occasionally, for 3 minutes, or until the fat begins to run. Add the onion and garlic and cook, stirring occasionally, for 5 minutes, or until softened.

3 Add the beef and cook, breaking it up with a wooden spoon, until browned all over. Stir in the celery and carrots and cook for 5 minutes. Season to taste with salt and pepper. Add the sugar, oregano and tomatoes. Bring to the boil, reduce the heat and simmer for 30 minutes.

4 Meanwhile, stir the mustard and Cheddar cheese into the béchamel sauce.

5 In a rectangular baking dish, make alternate layers of meat sauce, lasagne sheets and half the Parmesan cheese. Pour the béchamel sauce over the layers, covering them completely, and sprinkle with the remaining Parmesan cheese. Bake in the preheated oven for 30 minutes, or until golden brown and bubbling. Serve immediately.

lamb casserole with artichokes & olives

serves 4
- 4 tbsp Greek yogurt
- grated rind of 1 lemon
- 2 garlic cloves, crushed
- 3 tbsp olive oil
- 1 tsp ground cumin
- 700 g/1 lb 9 oz lean boneless lamb, cubed
- 1 onion, thinly sliced
- 150 ml/5 fl oz dry white wine
- 450 g/1 lb tomatoes, roughly chopped
- 1 tbsp tomato purée
- pinch of sugar
- 2 tbsp chopped fresh oregano or 1 tsp dried
- 2 bay leaves
- 85 g/3 oz kalamata olives
- 400 g/14 oz canned artichoke hearts, drained and halved
- salt and pepper

1 Put the yogurt, lemon rind, garlic, 1 tablespoon of the oil and cumin in a large bowl with salt and pepper to taste and mix together. Add the lamb and toss together until coated in the mixture. Cover and leave to marinate for at least 1 hour.

2 Heat 1 tablespoon of the remaining oil in a large flameproof casserole. Add the lamb, in batches, and fry for about 5 minutes, stirring frequently, until browned on all sides. Using a slotted spoon, remove the meat from the casserole. Add the remaining oil to the casserole with the onion and fry for 5 minutes, until softened.

3 Pour the wine into the casserole, stirring in any glazed bits from the bottom, and bring to the boil. Reduce the heat and return the meat to the casserole, then stir in the tomatoes, tomato purée, sugar, oregano and bay leaves.

4 Cover the casserole and simmer for about 1½ hours, until the lamb is tender. Stir in the olives and artichokes and simmer for a further 10 minutes. Remove the bay leaves and serve immediately.

lamb stew with sweet red peppers

serves 4

- 450 g/1 lb lean boneless lamb, such as leg or fillet
- 1½ tbsp plain flour
- 1 tsp ground cloves
- 1–1½ tbsp olive oil
- 1 onion, sliced
- 2–3 garlic cloves, sliced
- 300 ml/10 fl oz orange juice
- 150 ml/5 fl oz lamb or chicken stock
- 1 cinnamon stick, bruised
- 2 red peppers (sweet pointed variety, if available), deseeded and sliced into rings
- 4 tomatoes
- a few fresh coriander sprigs, plus 1 tbsp chopped fresh coriander to garnish
- salt and pepper

1 Preheat the oven to 190°C/375°F/Gas Mark 5.

2 Trim any fat or gristle from the lamb and cut into thin strips. Mix the flour and cloves together. Toss the lamb in the spiced flour until well coated and reserve any remaining spiced flour.

3 Heat 1 tablespoon of the oil in a heavy-based frying pan and cook the lamb over a high heat, stirring frequently, for 3 minutes, or until browned on all sides. Transfer to an ovenproof casserole.

4 Add the onion and garlic to the frying pan and cook over a medium heat, stirring frequently, for 3 minutes, adding the extra oil if necessary. Sprinkle in the reserved spiced flour and cook, stirring constantly, for 2 minutes, then remove from the heat.

5 Gradually stir in the orange juice and stock, then return to the heat and bring to the boil, stirring. Pour over the lamb in the casserole, add the cinnamon stick, red peppers, tomatoes and coriander sprigs and stir well. Cover and cook in the preheated oven for 1½ hours, or until the lamb is tender.

6 Discard the cinnamon stick and season to taste with salt and pepper. Serve immediately, garnished with the chopped coriander.

lamb shanks with gremolata

serves 4
- 4 lamb shanks
- 2 tbsp olive oil
- 4 garlic cloves, halved
- 1 dried chilli, crushed
- 3 fresh rosemary sprigs
- 6 ripe plum tomatoes
- 2 large onions, finely chopped
- 4 strips of orange zest
- 2 bay leaves
- 1 tsp brown sugar
- 100 ml/3½ fl oz red wine
- 500 ml/18 fl oz water
- salt and pepper

gremolata
- 100 g/3½ oz blanched almonds
- 2 garlic cloves, finely chopped
- grated rind of 2 lemons
- small bunch of fresh flat-leaf parsley, chopped

1 Preheat the oven to 180°C/350°F/Gas Mark 4. Season the lamb well with salt and pepper. Heat half the oil in a flameproof casserole. Add the lamb to the casserole and brown for 3 minutes on all sides, then remove from the heat. Chop the garlic, chilli and rosemary together.

2 Cut the tomatoes in half and, with the skin side in your hand, grate the flesh to form a rough tomato pulp. The skin will be left in your hand.

3 Remove the meat from the casserole and return the casserole to the heat with the remaining oil. Add the garlic, chilli and rosemary and fry for 2 minutes, until fragrant and aromatic. Add the onions and cook for about 5 minutes, until soft. Season to taste with salt and pepper.

4 Return the meat to the casserole with the orange zest, bay leaves, sugar, tomato pulp, wine and water. Cover and bring to a simmer, then transfer to the preheated oven and cook for 2½ hours, basting regularly.

5 Meanwhile, roast the almonds in the oven until golden brown. Leave to cool. When ready to serve, roughly chop the almonds and place in a bowl with the garlic, lemon rind and parsley. Mix well. Transfer the lamb shanks to serving plates and scatter over a little of the gremolata. Serve immediately.

turkish lamb casserole

serves 4
- 2 tbsp olive oil
- 4 lamb shanks, about 300 g/10½ oz each
- 2 onions, sliced
- 2 peppers, any colour, deseeded and chopped
- 2 garlic cloves, well crushed
- 1 aubergine, cut into small cubes
- ½ tsp paprika
- ½ tsp ground cinnamon
- 200 g/7 oz cooked chickpeas
- 400 g/14 oz canned chopped tomatoes
- 2 tsp mixed dried Mediterranean herbs
- 100 ml/3½ fl oz lamb or vegetable stock, plus extra if needed
- salt and pepper
- cooked couscous, to serve

1 Preheat the oven to 160°C/325°F/Gas Mark 3.

2 Heat half the oil in a large frying pan over a high heat, add the lamb shanks and cook, turning frequently, for 2–3 minutes, until browned all over. Transfer to a casserole.

3 Heat the remaining oil in the frying pan over a medium–high heat, add the onions and peppers and cook, stirring frequently, for 10–15 minutes, or until soft and just turning golden. Add the garlic, aubergine and spices and cook, stirring constantly, for 1 minute. Add the chickpeas, tomatoes, herbs and stock, stir well and bring to a simmer. Season to taste with salt and pepper and transfer to the casserole.

4 Cover the casserole, transfer to the preheated oven and cook for 1½ hours. Check after 45 minutes that the casserole is gently bubbling and that there is enough liquid – if it looks rather dry, add a little more stock and stir in. Serve immediately with couscous.

mediterranean lamb casserole

serves 4

- pinch of saffron threads
- 2 tbsp boiling water
- 450 g/1 lb lean boneless lamb, such as leg steaks
- 1½ tbsp plain flour
- 1 tsp ground coriander
- ½ tsp ground cumin
- ½ tsp ground allspice
- 1 tbsp olive oil
- 1 onion, chopped
- 2–3 garlic cloves, chopped
- 450 ml/16 fl oz lamb or chicken stock
- 1 cinnamon stick, bruised
- 85 g/3 oz dried apricots, roughly chopped
- 175 g/6 oz courgettes, sliced
- 115 g/4 oz cherry tomatoes
- 1 tbsp chopped fresh coriander
- salt and pepper
- 2 tbsp roughly chopped pistachio nuts, to garnish
- cooked couscous, to serve

1 Put the saffron threads in a heatproof jug with the water and leave for at least 10 minutes to infuse.

2 Trim off any fat or gristle from the lamb and cut into 2.5-cm/1-inch chunks. Mix the flour and spices together, then toss the lamb in the spiced flour until well coated and reserve any remaining spiced flour.

3 Heat the oil in a large heavy-based saucepan and cook the onion and garlic, stirring frequently, for 5 minutes, or until softened. Add the lamb and cook over a high heat, stirring frequently, for 3 minutes, or until browned on all sides. Sprinkle in the reserved spiced flour and cook, stirring constantly, for 2 minutes, then remove from the heat.

4 Gradually stir in the stock and the saffron and its soaking liquid, then return to the heat and bring to the boil, stirring. Add the cinnamon stick and apricots. Reduce the heat, cover and simmer, stirring occasionally, for 1 hour.

5 Add the courgettes and tomatoes and cook for a further 15 minutes. Discard the cinnamon stick. Stir in the fresh coriander and season to taste with salt and pepper. Serve immediately, sprinkled with the pistachio nuts and accompanied by couscous.

tagine of lamb

serves 4

- 1 tbsp sunflower or corn oil
- 1 onion, chopped
- 350 g/12 oz boneless lamb, trimmed of all visible fat and cut into 2.5-cm/1-inch cubes
- 1 garlic clove, finely chopped
- 600 ml/1 pint vegetable stock
- grated rind and juice of 1 orange
- 1 tsp honey
- 1 cinnamon stick
- 1-cm/½-inch piece fresh ginger, finely chopped
- 1 aubergine
- 4 tomatoes, peeled and chopped
- 115 g/4 oz ready-to-eat dried apricots
- 2 tbsp chopped fresh coriander
- salt and pepper
- cooked couscous, to serve

1 Heat the oil in a large heavy-based frying pan or flameproof casserole over a medium heat. Add the onion and lamb and cook, stirring frequently, for 5 minutes, or until the meat is lightly browned all over.

2 Add the garlic, stock, orange rind and juice, honey, cinnamon stick and ginger. Bring to the boil, then reduce the heat, cover and leave to simmer for 45 minutes.

3 Using a sharp knife, halve the aubergine lengthways and slice thinly. Add to the frying pan with the tomatoes and apricots. Cover and cook for a further 45 minutes, or until the lamb is tender.

4 Stir in the coriander and season to taste with salt and pepper. Serve immediately with couscous.

french country casserole

serves 6

- 2 tbsp sunflower oil
- 2 kg/4 lb 8 oz boneless leg of lamb, cut into 2.5-cm/1-inch cubes
- 6 leeks, sliced
- 1 tbsp plain flour
- 150 ml/5 fl oz rosé wine
- 300 ml/10 fl oz chicken stock
- 1 tbsp tomato purée
- 1 tbsp sugar
- 2 tbsp chopped fresh mint, plus extra sprigs to garnish
- 115 g/4 oz dried apricots, chopped
- 1 kg/2 lb 4 oz potatoes, sliced
- 3 tbsp melted unsalted butter
- salt and pepper

1 Preheat the oven to 180°C/350°F/Gas Mark 4.

2 Heat the oil in a large flameproof casserole. Add the lamb, in batches, and cook over a medium heat, stirring, for 5–8 minutes, or until browned all over. Transfer to a plate.

3 Add the leeks to the casserole and cook, stirring occasionally, for 5 minutes, or until softened. Sprinkle in the flour and cook, stirring, for 1 minute. Pour in the wine and stock and bring to the boil, stirring. Stir in the tomato purée, sugar, chopped mint and apricots and season to taste with salt and pepper.

4 Return the lamb to the casserole and stir. Arrange the potato slices on top and brush with the melted butter. Cover and bake in the preheated oven for 1½ hours.

5 Increase the oven temperature to 200°C/400°F/Gas Mark 6, uncover the casserole and bake for a further 30 minutes, or until the potato topping is golden brown. Serve immediately, garnished with mint sprigs.

lamb stew with chickpeas

serves 6

- 6 tbsp olive oil
- 225 g/8 oz chorizo sausage, cut into 5 mm/¼ inch thick slices, casings removed
- 2 large onions, chopped
- 6 large garlic cloves, crushed
- 900 g/2 lb boneless leg of lamb, cut into 5 cm/2 inch chunks
- 250 ml/9 fl oz lamb stock or water
- 125 ml/4 fl oz red wine, such as Rioja or Tempranillo
- 2 tbsp sherry vinegar
- 800 g/1 lb 12 oz canned chopped tomatoes
- 4 fresh thyme sprigs, plus extra to garnish
- 2 bay leaves
- ½ tsp sweet paprika
- 800 g/1 lb 12 oz canned chickpeas, drained and rinsed
- salt and pepper

1 Preheat the oven to 160°C/325°F/Gas Mark 3.

2 Heat 4 tablespoons of the oil in a large flameproof casserole over a medium–high heat. Reduce the heat, add the chorizo and fry for 1 minute. Transfer to a plate. Add the onions to the casserole and fry for 2 minutes, then add the garlic and continue cooking for 3 minutes, or until the onions are soft but not brown. Remove from the casserole and set aside.

3 Heat the remaining oil in the casserole. Add the lamb, in batches if necessary, and cook, stirring, for 5 minutes, until browned on all sides.

4 Return the onion mixture and chorizo to the casserole with the lamb. Stir in the stock, wine, vinegar, tomatoes and salt and pepper to taste. Bring to the boil, scraping any glazed bits from the base of the casserole. Reduce the heat and stir in the thyme sprigs, bay leaves and paprika.

5 Transfer to the preheated oven and cook, covered, for 40–45 minutes, until the lamb is tender. Stir in the chickpeas and return to the oven, uncovered, for 10 minutes.

6 Taste and adjust the seasoning, adding salt and pepper if needed. Serve immediately, garnished with thyme sprigs.

pasticcio

serves 4

- 1 tbsp olive oil
- 1 onion, chopped
- 2 garlic cloves, finely chopped
- 450 g/1 lb fresh lamb mince
- 2 tbsp tomato purée
- 2 tbsp plain flour
- 300 ml/10 fl oz chicken stock
- 1 tsp ground cinnamon
- 115 g/4 oz dried macaroni
- 2 beef tomatoes, sliced
- 300 ml/10 fl oz Greek yogurt
- 2 eggs, lightly beaten
- salt and pepper

1 Preheat the oven to 190°C/375°F/Gas Mark 5.

2 Heat the oil in a large heavy-based frying pan. Add the onion and garlic and cook over a low heat, stirring occasionally, for 5 minutes, or until softened. Add the lamb and cook, breaking it up with a wooden spoon, until browned all over.

3 Add the tomato purée and sprinkle in the flour. Cook, stirring, for 1 minute, then stir in the stock. Season to taste with salt and pepper and stir in the cinnamon. Bring to the boil, reduce the heat, cover and cook for 25 minutes.

4 Meanwhile, bring a large heavy-based saucepan of lightly salted water to the boil. Add the pasta, return to the boil and cook for 8–10 minutes, or until tender but still firm to the bite.

5 Drain the pasta and stir into the lamb mixture. Spoon into a large ovenproof dish and arrange the tomato slices on top. Beat together the yogurt and eggs, then spoon over the lamb evenly. Bake in the preheated oven for 1 hour, or until the topping is golden brown. Serve imrnediately.

lamb & potato moussaka

serves 4

- 1 large aubergine, sliced
- 1 tbsp olive oil
- 1 onion, finely chopped
- 1 garlic clove, crushed
- 350 g/12 oz fresh lean lamb mince
- 250 g/9 oz mushrooms, sliced
- 425 g/15 oz canned chopped tomatoes with herbs
- 150 ml/5 fl oz lamb stock
- 2 tbsp cornflour
- 2 tbsp water
- 500 g/1 lb 2 oz potatoes, parboiled for 10 minutes and sliced
- 2 eggs
- 125 g/4½ oz low-fat soft cheese
- 150 ml/5 fl oz low-fat natural yogurt
- 55 g/2 oz mature Cheddar cheese, grated
- salt and pepper

1 Preheat the oven to 190°C/375°F/Gas Mark 5.

2 Lay the aubergine slices on a clean board and sprinkle with salt. Leave for 10 minutes, then turn the slices over and repeat. Place in a colander, rinse and drain.

3 Meanwhile, heat the oil in a large saucepan. Add the onion and garlic and cook for 3–4 minutes. Add the lamb and mushrooms and cook over a medium heat for 5 minutes, or until browned. Stir in the tomatoes and stock, bring to the boil and simmer for 10 minutes. Mix the cornflour and water together to make a smooth paste, then stir into the saucepan. Cook, stirring constantly, until thickened.

4 Spoon half the mixture into an ovenproof dish. Cover with the aubergine slices, then the remaining lamb mixture. Arrange the sliced potatoes on top.

5 Beat the eggs, soft cheese and yogurt together. Season to taste with salt and pepper, then pour over the potatoes to cover. Sprinkle over the cheese and bake in the preheated oven for 45 minutes, or until the topping is golden brown. Serve immediately.

Mmmm...

pork stroganoff

serves 4
- 350 g/12 oz lean pork fillet
- 1 tbsp vegetable oil
- 1 onion, chopped
- 2 garlic cloves, crushed
- 25 g/1 oz plain flour
- 2 tbsp tomato purée
- 425 ml/15 fl oz chicken or vegetable stock
- 125 g/4½ oz button mushrooms, sliced
- 1 large green pepper, deseeded and chopped
- ½ tsp freshly grated nutmeg, plus extra to garnish
- 4 tbsp low-fat natural yogurt, plus extra to serve
- salt and pepper
- cooked rice, to serve
- chopped fresh parsley, to garnish

1 Trim off any fat or gristle from the pork and cut into 1 cm/½ inch thick slices. Heat the oil in a large heavy-based frying pan and gently fry the pork, onion and garlic for 4–5 minutes, or until lightly browned.

2 Stir in the flour and tomato purée, then pour in the stock and stir to mix thoroughly. Add the mushrooms, green pepper and nutmeg with salt and pepper to taste. Bring to the boil, cover and simmer for 20 minutes, or until the pork is tender and cooked through.

3 Remove the frying pan from the heat and stir in the yogurt. Transfer to warmed serving plates. Serve immediately with rice and an extra spoonful of yogurt and garnish with parsley and nutmeg.

pork & vegetable stew

serves 4

- 450 g/1 lb lean pork fillet
- 1½ tbsp plain flour
- 1 tsp ground coriander
- 1 tsp ground cumin
- 1½ tsp ground cinnamon
- 1 tbsp olive oil
- 1 onion, chopped
- 400 g/14 oz canned chopped tomatoes
- 2 tbsp tomato purée
- 300–450 ml/10–16 fl oz chicken stock
- 225 g/8 oz carrots, chopped
- 350 g/12 oz squash, such as kabocha, peeled, deseeded and chopped
- 225 g/8 oz leeks, sliced, blanched and drained
- 115 g/4 oz okra, trimmed and sliced
- salt and pepper
- fresh parsley sprigs, to garnish
- cooked couscous, to serve

1 Trim off any fat or gristle from the pork and cut into thin strips about 5 cm/2 inches long. Mix the flour and spices together. Toss the pork in the spiced flour until well coated and reserve any remaining spiced flour.

2 Heat the oil in a large heavy-based saucepan and cook the onion, stirring frequently, for 5 minutes, or until softened. Add the pork and cook over a high heat, stirring frequently, for 5 minutes, or until browned on all sides. Sprinkle in the reserved spiced flour and cook, stirring constantly, for 2 minutes, then remove from the heat.

3 Gradually add the tomatoes to the saucepan. Blend the tomato purée with a little of the stock in a jug and gradually stir into the saucepan, then stir in half the remaining stock.

4 Add the carrots, then return to the heat and bring to the boil, stirring. Reduce the heat, cover and simmer, stirring occasionally, for 1½ hours. Add the squash and cook for a further 15 minutes.

5 Add the leeks and okra, and the remaining stock if you prefer a thinner stew. Simmer for a further 15 minutes, or until the pork and vegetables are tender. Season to taste with salt and pepper, garnish with parsley sprigs and serve immediately with couscous.

pork hotpot

serves 6

- 85 g/3 oz plain flour
- 1.3 kg/3 lb pork fillet, cut into 5-mm/¼-inch slices
- 4 tbsp sunflower oil
- 2 onions, thinly sliced
- 2 garlic cloves, finely chopped
- 400 g/14 oz canned chopped tomatoes
- 350 ml/12 fl oz dry white wine
- 1 tbsp torn fresh basil leaves
- 2 tbsp chopped fresh parsley
- salt and pepper
- fresh oregano sprigs, to garnish
- fresh crusty bread, to serve

1 Spread the flour on a plate and season well with salt and pepper. Coat the pork slices in the flour, shaking off any excess. Heat the oil in a flameproof casserole. Add the pork slices and cook over a medium heat, turning occasionally, for 4–5 minutes, or until browned all over. Transfer the pork to a plate with a slotted spoon.

2 Add the onions to the casserole and cook over a low heat, stirring occasionally, for 10 minutes, or until golden brown. Add the garlic and cook for a further 2 minutes, then add the tomatoes, wine and basil and season to taste with salt and pepper. Cook, stirring frequently, for 3 minutes.

3 Return the pork to the casserole, cover and simmer gently for 1 hour, or until the meat is tender. Stir in the parsley, garnish with oregano sprigs and serve immediately with crusty bread.

classic french cassoulet

serves 8

- 500 g/1 lb 2 oz dried haricot beans, soaked overnight
- bouquet garni
- 1 celery stick, roughly chopped
- 3 onions, 1 quartered, 2 thinly sliced
- 4 large garlic cloves, 2 whole, 2 chopped
- 2 litres/3½ pints water
- 500 g/1 lb 2 oz pork belly, skin removed
- 2 tbsp duck fat or vegetable oil
- 400 g/14 oz Toulouse or pork sausage
- 400 g/14 oz lamb shoulder, boned and cut into 4 large chunks
- 2 tbsp tomato purée
- 150 g/5½ oz fresh breadcrumbs
- green salad, to serve

1 Drain and rinse the beans and put them in a large saucepan with the bouquet garni, celery, onion quarters and whole garlic cloves. Add the water and bring to the boil. Skim off any foam, then reduce the heat to low. Gently simmer for 1 hour, uncovered.

2 Meanwhile, cut the pork belly into 4-cm/1½-inch pieces, then add the duck fat to a large heavy-based saucepan and place over a high heat. Add the pork belly and cook until browned all over. Remove and reserve, then repeat with the sausages, then the lamb. Add the sliced onions, chopped garlic and tomato purée and cook in the remaining fat for 2 minutes. Remove from the heat and leave to cool.

3 Preheat the oven to 180°C/350°F/Gas Mark 4.

4 Drain the beans, reserving the liquid but discarding the vegetables. In a large casserole, layer the beans and meat alternately until they're all used up. Add the onion mixture and enough of the bean-cooking liquid to almost cover. Sprinkle over the breadcrumbs, cover and cook in the preheated oven for 1 hour. Reduce the heat to 140°C/275°F/Gas Mark 1, uncover and cook for a further hour.

5 Make sure that the cassoulet isn't too dry, adding a little heated bean liquid or water if necessary. Serve immediately with a green salad.

catalan pork stew

serves 4–6
- 2 tbsp olive oil
- 2 kg/4 lb 8 oz boneless pork shoulder, cut into 7.5-cm/3-inch chunks
- bouquet garni
- 750 ml/1⅓ pints white wine
- 3–4 carrots, cut into 1-cm/½-inch slices
- 800 g/1 lb 12 oz canned chickpeas, drained and rinsed
- salt and pepper

sofregit
- 2 onions, chopped
- 125 ml/4 fl oz olive oil
- 4 large tomatoes, grated, skins and cores discarded
- 4 large garlic cloves, finely chopped
- 1 tbsp hot paprika

picada
- 1 slice day-old country bread, about 30 g/1 oz, fried in olive oil
- 1 tbsp blanched almonds, toasted
- 1 tbsp skinned hazelnuts, toasted
- 2 garlic cloves, crushed
- 30 g/1 oz plain chocolate
- olive oil, as required

1 For the sofregit, put the onions and oil in a large saucepan and place over a medium–high heat. Cook, stirring occasionally, for 10 minutes. Reduce the heat to very low and cook for a further 10–20 minutes, until golden brown. Add the tomatoes, garlic and paprika, and simmer, stirring, for 15 minutes.

2 Preheat the oven to 160°C/325°F/Gas Mark 3. Pour the oil into a flameproof casserole and heat over a medium–high heat. Brown the pork on all sides in batches, adding more oil if necessary. Pour off any excess fat. Stir in the sofregit, bouquet garni, and salt and pepper to taste. Pour in the wine and enough water to cover, then bring to the boil. Cover and bake in the preheated oven for 1¼ hours. Stir in the carrots, re-cover the casserole and return to the oven for 30 minutes, or until the pork and carrots are tender.

3 Meanwhile, to make the picada, tear the bread into a food processor, then add the almonds, hazelnuts, garlic and chocolate and process until finely blended. With the motor running, slowly pour in enough oil to form a thick paste.

4 Transfer the casserole to the hob. Remove the pork and carrots with a slotted spoon and set aside. Bring the cooking liquid to the boil and place several ladlefuls in a heatproof bowl. Stir in the picada until well blended, then stir this mixture into the casserole and boil for 2 minutes. Reduce the heat and add the pork, carrots and chickpeas. Simmer for about 5 minutes, or until the stew thickens. Serve immediately.

pot-roast pork

serves 4

- 1 tbsp sunflower oil
- 55 g/2 oz butter
- 1 kg/2 lb 4 oz boned and rolled pork loin joint
- 4 shallots, chopped
- 6 juniper berries
- 2 fresh thyme sprigs, plus extra to garnish
- 150 ml/5 fl oz dry cider
- 150 ml/5 fl oz chicken stock or water
- 8 celery sticks, chopped
- 2 tbsp plain flour
- 150 ml/5 fl oz double cream
- salt and pepper

1 Heat the oil with half the butter in a large heavy-based saucepan or flameproof casserole. Add the pork and cook over a medium heat, turning frequently, for 5–10 minutes, or until browned. Transfer to a plate.

2 Add the shallots to the saucepan and cook, stirring frequently, for 5 minutes, or until softened. Add the juniper berries and thyme sprigs and return the pork to the saucepan with any juices that have collected on the plate. Pour in the cider and stock, season to taste with salt and pepper, then cover and simmer for 30 minutes. Turn the pork over and add the celery. Re-cover the pan and cook for a further 40 minutes.

3 Meanwhile, make a beurre manié by mashing the remaining butter with the flour in a small bowl. Transfer the pork and celery to a platter with a slotted spoon and keep warm. Remove and discard the juniper berries and thyme. Whisk the beurre manié, a little at a time, into the simmering cooking liquid. Cook, stirring constantly, for 2 minutes, then stir in the cream and bring to the boil.

4 Slice the pork and spoon a little of the sauce over it. Garnish with thyme sprigs and serve immediately. Hand around the remaining sauce separately.

ham stew with black-eyed beans

serves 4

- 450–550 g/1–1 lb 4 oz lean gammon
- 2½ tbsp olive oil
- 1 onion, chopped
- 2–3 garlic cloves, chopped
- 2 celery sticks, chopped
- 175 g/6 oz carrots, sliced
- 1 cinnamon stick, bruised
- ½ tsp ground cloves
- ¼ tsp freshly grated nutmeg
- 1 tsp dried oregano
- 450 ml/16 fl oz chicken stock or vegetable stock
- 1–2 tbsp maple syrup
- 3 large spicy sausages, or about 225 g/8 oz chorizo
- 400 g/14 oz canned black-eyed beans, drained and rinsed
- 1 orange pepper, deseeded and chopped
- 1 tbsp cornflour
- 2 tbsp water
- pepper

1 Trim off any fat or skin from the gammon and cut into 4-cm/1½-inch chunks. Heat 1 tablespoon of the oil in a heavy-based saucepan or flameproof casserole and cook the gammon over a high heat, stirring frequently, for 5 minutes, or until browned on all sides. Using a slotted spoon, remove from the saucepan and set aside.

2 Add the onion, garlic, celery and carrots to the saucepan with 1 tablespoon of the remaining oil and cook over a medium heat, stirring frequently, for 5 minutes, or until softened. Add all the spices, season to taste with pepper and cook, stirring constantly, for 2 minutes.

3 Return the gammon to the saucepan. Add the oregano, stock and maple syrup to taste, then bring to the boil, stirring. Reduce the heat, cover and simmer, stirring occasionally, for 1 hour.

4 Heat the remaining oil in a frying pan and cook the sausages, turning frequently, until browned all over. Remove and cut each into 3–4 chunks, then add to the saucepan. Add the beans and orange pepper and simmer for a further 20 minutes. Blend the cornflour with the water and stir into the stew, then cook for 3–5 minutes. Serve immediately.

pork, sausage & rice bake

serves 4

- 2 tbsp sunflower oil
- 25 g/1 oz butter
- 450 g/1 lb pork fillet or loin, cut into thin strips
- 1 large onion, chopped
- 1 red pepper, deseeded and sliced
- 1 orange pepper, deseeded and sliced
- 115 g/4 oz mushrooms, sliced
- 140 g/5 oz long-grain rice
- 425 ml/15 fl oz beef stock
- 225 g/8 oz smoked sausage, sliced
- ¼ tsp ground mixed spice
- salt and pepper
- 2 tbsp chopped fresh parsley, to garnish

1 Preheat the oven to 180°C/350°F/Gas Mark 4.

2 Heat the oil and butter in a large flameproof casserole. Add the pork and cook over a medium heat, stirring, for 5 minutes, until browned. Transfer to a plate.

3 Add the onion and cook over a low heat, stirring occasionally, for 5 minutes, or until softened. Add the red and orange peppers and cook, stirring frequently, for a further 4–5 minutes. Add the mushrooms and cook for 1 minute, then stir in the rice. Cook for 1 minute, or until the grains are well coated, then add the stock and bring to the boil.

4 Return the pork to the casserole, add the sausage and mixed spice and season to taste with salt and pepper. Mix thoroughly, cover and cook in the preheated oven for 1 hour, or until all the liquid has been absorbed and the meat is tender. Serve immediately, garnished with the parsley.

pork & pasta bake

serves 4

- 2 tbsp olive oil
- 1 onion, chopped
- 1 garlic clove, finely chopped
- 2 carrots, diced
- 55 g/2 oz pancetta, chopped
- 115 g/4 oz mushrooms, chopped
- 450 g/1 lb fresh pork mince
- 125 ml/4 fl oz dry white wine
- 4 tbsp passata
- 200 g/7 oz canned chopped tomatoes
- 2 tsp chopped fresh sage, plus extra sprigs to garnish
- 225 g/8 oz dried penne
- 140 g/5 oz mozzarella cheese, diced
- 4 tbsp freshly grated Parmesan cheese
- 300 ml/10 fl oz béchamel sauce (see page 9)
- salt and pepper

1 Preheat the oven to 200°C/400°F/Gas Mark 6.

2 Heat the oil in a large heavy-based frying pan. Add the onion, garlic and carrots and cook over a low heat, stirring occasionally, for 5 minutes, or until the onion has softened. Add the pancetta and cook for 5 minutes. Add the mushrooms and cook, stirring occasionally, for a further 2 minutes. Add the pork and cook, breaking it up with a wooden spoon, until the meat is browned all over. Stir in the wine, passata, tomatoes and chopped sage. Season to taste with salt and pepper, bring to the boil, then cover and simmer over a low heat for 25–30 minutes.

3 Meanwhile, bring a large heavy-based saucepan of lightly salted water to the boil. Add the pasta, return to the boil and cook for 8–10 minutes, or until tender but still firm to the bite.

4 Spoon the pork mixture into a large ovenproof dish. Stir the mozzarella and half the Parmesan into the béchamel sauce. Drain the pasta and stir into the sauce, then spoon over the pork mixture. Sprinkle with the remaining Parmesan and bake in the preheated oven for 25–30 minutes, or until golden brown. Serve immediately, garnished with sage sprigs.

Mmmm...
poultry

coq au vin

serves 4

- 25 g/1 oz butter
- 8 baby onions
- 125 g/4½ oz streaky bacon, roughly chopped
- 4 chicken portions
- 1 garlic clove, finely chopped
- 12 button mushrooms
- 300 ml/10 fl oz full-bodied red wine
- bouquet garni
- 1 tbsp chopped fresh tarragon
- 2 tsp cornflour
- 1–2 tbsp cold water
- salt and pepper
- chopped fresh flat-leaf parsley, to garnish

1 Melt half of the butter in a large frying pan over a medium heat. Add the onions and bacon and cook, stirring, for 3 minutes. Lift out the bacon and onions and reserve.

2 Melt the remaining butter in the frying pan and add the chicken portions. Cook for 3 minutes, then turn over and cook on the other side for 2 minutes. Drain off some of the chicken fat before returning the bacon and onions to the pan. Add the garlic, mushrooms, wine, bouquet garni and tarragon. Season to taste with salt and pepper. Cook for about 1 hour, or until the juices run clear when a skewer is inserted into the thickest part of the meat.

3 Remove the frying pan from the heat, lift out the chicken, onions, bacon and mushrooms with a slotted spoon, transfer them to a serving platter and keep warm. Discard the bouquet garni.

4 Mix the cornflour with enough of the water to make a paste, then stir into the juices in the frying pan. Bring to the boil, reduce the heat and cook, stirring, for 1 minute. Pour the sauce over the chicken and serve immediately, garnished with parsley.

chicken casserole with dumplings

serves 4

- 4 chicken quarters
- 2 tbsp sunflower oil
- 2 leeks, trimmed and sliced
- 250 g/9 oz carrots, chopped
- 250 g/9 oz parsnips, chopped
- 2 small turnips, chopped
- 600 ml/1 pint chicken stock
- 3 tbsp Worcestershire sauce
- 2 fresh rosemary sprigs
- salt and pepper

dumplings

- 200 g/7 oz self-raising flour
- 100 g/3½ oz suet
- 1 tbsp chopped fresh rosemary leaves
- salt and pepper

1 Remove the skin from the chicken if you prefer. Heat the oil in a large flameproof casserole or heavy-based saucepan over a medium–high heat and fry the chicken until golden. Using a slotted spoon, remove the chicken from the casserole. Drain off the excess fat.

2 Add the leeks, carrots, parsnips and turnips to the casserole and cook for 5 minutes, until lightly coloured. Return the chicken to the casserole. Add the stock, Worcestershire sauce and rosemary sprigs with salt and pepper to taste, then bring to the boil. Reduce the heat, cover and simmer gently for about 50 minutes, or until the juices run clear when a skewer is inserted into the thickest part of the meat.

3 To make the dumplings, combine the flour, suet, chopped rosemary and salt and pepper to taste in a bowl. Stir in just enough cold water to bind to a firm dough.

4 Form into 8 small balls and place on top of the chicken and vegetables. Cover and simmer for a further 10–12 minutes, until the dumplings are well risen. Serve immediately.

chicken, tomato & onion casserole

serves 4
- 1½ tbsp unsalted butter
- 2 tbsp olive oil
- 450 g/1 lb skinless chicken drumsticks
- 2 red onions, sliced
- 2 garlic cloves, finely chopped
- 400 g/14 oz canned chopped tomatoes
- 2 tbsp chopped fresh flat-leaf parsley, plus extra to garnish
- 6 fresh basil leaves, torn
- 1 tbsp sun-dried tomato purée
- 150 ml/5 fl oz full-bodied red wine
- 225 g/8 oz mushrooms, sliced
- salt and pepper

1 Preheat the oven to 160°C/325°F/Gas Mark 3.

2 Heat the butter with the oil in a large flameproof casserole. Add the chicken drumsticks and cook, turning frequently, for 5–10 minutes, or until browned all over. Using a slotted spoon, transfer the drumsticks to a plate.

3 Add the onions and garlic to the casserole and cook over a low heat, stirring occasionally, for 10 minutes, or until golden. Add the tomatoes, parsley, basil, sun-dried tomato purée and wine, and season to taste with salt and pepper. Bring to the boil, then return the chicken drumsticks to the casserole, pushing them down under the liquid.

4 Cover and cook in the preheated oven for 50 minutes. Add the mushrooms and cook for a further 10 minutes, or until the chicken drumsticks are tender and the juices run clear when a skewer is inserted into the thickest part of the meat. Serve immediately, garnished with parsley.

chicken with 40 garlic cloves

serves 4

- 1.5–2 kg/3 lb 5 oz–4 lb 8 oz whole chicken
- ½ lemon
- 40 whole garlic cloves, peeled
- 2 tbsp olive oil
- 4 fresh thyme sprigs
- 2 fresh rosemary sprigs
- 4 fresh parsley sprigs
- 1 large carrot, roughly chopped
- 2 celery sticks, roughly chopped
- 1 onion, roughly chopped
- 375 ml/13 fl oz white wine
- salt and pepper
- crusty French bread and a green salad, to serve

1 Preheat the oven to 200°C/400°F/Gas Mark 6.

2 Stuff the chicken with the ½ lemon and 4 of the garlic cloves. Rub the chicken with a little of the oil and some salt and pepper.

3 In a large flameproof casserole, spread out the remaining garlic cloves, the herbs, carrot, celery and onion, then place the chicken on top. Pour over the remaining oil and add the wine. Cover with a tight-fitting lid, place in the preheated oven and bake for 1¼ hours.

4 Remove the chicken from the casserole and check that it's cooked by inserting a skewer into the thickest part of the meat; the juices should run clear. Cover and keep warm. Remove the garlic cloves and reserve.

5 Place the casserole over a low heat and simmer the juices for 5 minutes to make a gravy. Strain, reserving the vegetables.

6 Carve the chicken and serve it with the vegetables from the casserole. Squeeze the flesh out of the garlic cloves and spread it on the bread. Serve immediately, accompanied by a green salad.

chicken & barley stew

serves 4

- 2 tbsp vegetable oil
- 8 small skinless chicken thighs
- 500 ml/18 fl oz chicken stock
- 100 g/3½ oz pearl barley, rinsed and drained
- 200 g/7 oz small new potatoes, scrubbed and halved lengthways
- 2 large carrots, sliced
- 1 leek, trimmed and sliced
- 2 shallots, sliced
- 1 tbsp tomato purée
- 1 bay leaf
- 1 courgette, trimmed and sliced
- 2 tbsp chopped fresh flat-leaf parsley, plus extra sprigs to garnish
- 2 tbsp plain flour
- 4 tbsp water
- salt and pepper

1 Heat the oil in a large saucepan over a medium heat. Add the chicken and cook for 3 minutes, then turn over and cook on the other side for a further 2 minutes. Add the stock, barley, potatoes, carrots, leek, shallots, tomato purée and bay leaf. Bring to the boil, reduce the heat and simmer for 30 minutes.

2 Add the courgette and chopped parsley, cover the pan and cook for a further 20 minutes, or until the juices run clear when a skewer is inserted into the thickest part of the meat. Remove the bay leaf and discard.

3 In a separate bowl, mix the flour with the water and stir into a smooth paste. Add it to the pan and cook, stirring, over a low heat for a further 5 minutes. Season to taste with salt and pepper.

4 Remove from the heat, ladle into individual serving bowls and garnish with parsley sprigs. Serve immediately.

chicken, pumpkin & chorizo casserole

serves 4

- 3 tbsp olive oil
- 2.25 kg/5 lb chicken, cut into 8 pieces and dusted in flour
- 200 g/7 oz fresh chorizo sausages, roughly sliced
- small bunch of fresh sage leaves
- 1 onion, chopped
- 6 garlic cloves, sliced
- 2 celery sticks, sliced
- 1 small pumpkin or butternut squash, peeled, deseeded and roughly chopped
- 200 ml/7 fl oz dry sherry
- 600 ml/1 pint chicken stock
- 400 g/14 oz chopped tomatoes
- 2 bay leaves
- 1 tbsp chopped fresh flat-leaf parsley
- salt and pepper

1 Preheat the oven to 180°C/350°F/Gas Mark 4.

2 Heat the oil in a flameproof casserole and cook the chicken, in batches, with the chorizo and sage leaves, until golden brown. Remove with a slotted spoon and reserve.

3 Add the onion, garlic, celery and pumpkin to the casserole and cook for 20 minutes, or until the mixture is golden brown.

4 Add the sherry, stock, tomatoes and bay leaves, and season to taste with salt and pepper. Return the reserved chicken, chorizo and sage to the casserole. Cover and cook in the preheated oven for 1 hour.

5 Remove from the oven, stir in the parsley and serve immediately.

chicken & butternut squash casserole

serves 4

- 2 tbsp olive oil
- 4 skinless, boneless chicken thighs, about 100 g/3½ oz each, cut into bite-sized pieces
- 1 large onion, sliced
- 2 leeks, chopped
- 2 garlic cloves, chopped
- 1 butternut squash, peeled, deseeded and cut into cubes
- 2 carrots, diced
- 400 g/14 oz canned chopped tomatoes with herbs
- 400 g/14 oz canned mixed beans, drained and rinsed
- 100 ml/3½ fl oz vegetable or chicken stock, plus extra if needed
- salt and pepper

1 Preheat the oven to 160°C/325°F/Gas Mark 3.

2 Heat half the oil in a large flameproof casserole over a high heat, add the chicken and cook, turning frequently, for 2–3 minutes, until browned all over. Reduce the heat to medium, remove the chicken with a slotted spoon and set aside.

3 Add the remaining oil to the casserole, add the onion and leeks and cook, stirring occasionally, for 10 minutes, or until soft. Add the garlic, squash and carrots and cook, stirring, for 2 minutes. Add the tomatoes, beans and stock, stir well and bring to a simmer. Return the chicken to the casserole.

4 Cover, transfer to the preheated oven and cook for 1–1¼ hours, stirring once or twice. If the casserole looks too dry, add a little extra stock. Season to taste with salt and pepper and serve immediately.

garlic chicken casserole

serves 4

- 4 tbsp sunflower oil
- 900 g/2 lb skinless, boneless chicken breast, chopped
- 250 g/9 oz mushrooms, sliced
- 16 shallots
- 6 garlic cloves, crushed
- 1 tbsp plain flour
- 250 ml/9 fl oz dry white wine
- 250 ml/9 fl oz chicken stock
- bouquet garni
- 1 celery stick
- 400 g/14 oz canned borlotti beans, drained and rinsed
- salt and pepper
- steamed squash and crusty bread, to serve

1 Preheat the oven to 150°C/300°F/Gas Mark 2.

2 Heat the oil in a flameproof casserole and fry the chicken until browned all over. Using a slotted spoon, remove the chicken from the casserole and set aside until required.

3 Add the mushrooms, shallots and garlic to the casserole and cook for 4 minutes. Return the chicken to the casserole and sprinkle with the flour, then cook for a further 2 minutes.

4 Add the wine and stock, stir until boiling, then add the bouquet garni and celery stick. Season to taste with salt and pepper, then add the beans.

5 Cover and place in the centre of the preheated oven and cook for 2 hours. Discard the bouquet garni and celery stick and serve the casserole immediately with squash and bread.

chicken in riesling

serves 4–6

- 2 tbsp plain flour
- 1 whole chicken, weighing 1.6 kg/3 lb 8 oz, cut into 8 pieces, or 8 chicken thighs
- 55 g/2 oz unsalted butter
- 1 tbsp sunflower oil
- 4 shallots, finely chopped
- 12 button mushrooms, sliced
- 2 tbsp brandy
- 500 ml/18 fl oz Riesling wine
- 250 ml/9 fl oz double cream
- salt and pepper
- chopped fresh flat-leaf parsley, to serve

1 Season the flour with salt and pepper to taste and toss the chicken pieces in it to coat. Shake off any excess.

2 Melt 30 g/1 oz of the butter with the oil in a large flameproof casserole over a medium–high heat. Add the chicken pieces, in batches, and cook, turning frequently, until browned all over. Remove from the casserole and set aside.

3 Pour off all the fat and wipe the casserole with kitchen paper. Melt the remaining butter in the casserole, add the shallots and mushrooms and sauté, stirring constantly, for 3 minutes. Return the chicken to the casserole and remove from the heat.

4 Warm the brandy in a small saucepan, ignite and pour it over the chicken pieces to flambé. When the flames die down, return to the heat, pour in the wine and bring to the boil. Reduce the heat, cover and simmer for 40–45 minutes, until the chicken is tender and the juices run clear when a skewer is inserted into the thickest part of the meat. Transfer the chicken to a serving platter and keep warm.

5 Skim the fat from the surface of the cooking liquid. Stir in the cream, then bring to the boil and reduce by half. Season to taste with salt and pepper. Spoon the sauce over the chicken pieces and sprinkle with parsley. Serve immediately.

chicken biryani

serves 8

- small piece fresh ginger
- 1½ tsp crushed garlic
- 1 tbsp garam masala
- 1 tsp chilli powder
- 2 tsp salt
- 5 crushed cardamom pods
- 300 ml/10 fl oz natural yogurt
- 1.5 kg/3 lb 5 oz whole chicken
- 150 ml/5 fl oz milk
- 1½ tsp saffron strands
- 6 tbsp ghee
- 2 onions, sliced
- 450 g/1 lb basmati rice
- 2 cinnamon sticks
- 4 fresh green chillies, deseeded and chopped
- 2 tbsp chopped fresh coriander leaves
- 4 tbsp lemon juice

1 Finely chop the ginger, then place in a bowl with the garlic, garam masala, chilli powder, half the salt and the cardamom pods. Add the yogurt. Skin the chicken, cut into 8 pieces, then add the pieces to the yogurt mixture and mix well. Cover and leave to marinate in the refrigerator for 3 hours.

2 Pour the milk into a small saucepan and bring to the boil, then pour into a heatproof bowl and sprinkle over the saffron. Set aside.

3 Heat the ghee in a saucepan. Add the onions and fry until golden. Transfer half of the onions and ghee to a bowl and reserve.

4 Place the rice and cinnamon sticks in a saucepan of water. Bring to the boil and remove from the heat when the rice is half-cooked. Drain and place in a bowl. Mix with the remaining salt.

5 Add the chicken mixture to the saucepan containing the onions. Add half of the chillies, coriander, lemon juice and saffron milk. Add the rice, then the rest of the ingredients, including the reserved onions and ghee. Cover tightly. Cook over a low heat for 1 hour, until the juices run clear when a skewer is inserted into the thickest part of the chicken. Mix well and serve immediately.

chicken with apricots & chickpeas

serves 4

- 2 tbsp olive or sunflower oil
- 1 large whole chicken, cut into 8 pieces, or 8 chicken thighs
- 2 large onions, sliced
- 2 large garlic cloves, crushed
- 2 tsp ground coriander
- 1½ tsp ground ginger
- 1½ tsp ground cumin
- pinch of dried chilli flakes, to taste (optional)
- 400 g/14 oz dried apricots, soaked overnight in 300 ml/10 fl oz orange juice
- 400 g/14 oz canned chickpeas, drained and rinsed
- large pinch of saffron threads
- 1 preserved lemon, rinsed and sliced
- 30 g/1 oz flaked almonds, toasted
- fresh flat-leaf parsley sprigs, to garnish
- cooked couscous, to serve

1 Heat the oil in a flameproof casserole over a medium–high heat. Add as many chicken pieces as will fit without overcrowding and fry for 3–5 minutes, until golden brown. Remove from the casserole and set aside while you fry the remaining pieces.

2 Pour off all but 2 tablespoons of the oil from the casserole. Add the onions and stir for 4 minutes. Add the garlic and continue stirring for 1–2 minutes, until the onions are soft but not brown. Stir in the coriander, ginger, cumin and chilli flakes, if using, and cook, stirring, for 1 minute.

3 Return the chicken pieces to the casserole with enough water to cover. Bring to the boil, then reduce the heat and leave to simmer for 20 minutes. Add the apricots, chickpeas and saffron and continue to simmer for 10 minutes, or until the juices run clear when a skewer is inserted into the thickest part of the chicken.

4 Using a slotted spoon, transfer the chicken, apricots and chickpeas to a serving platter and keep warm. Bring the liquid in the casserole to the boil and reduce by half. Pour this liquid over the chicken, add the preserved lemon and sprinkle with the flaked almonds. Transfer to serving plates, garnish with parsley sprigs and serve immediately with couscous.

chicken & apple pot

serves 4
- 1 tbsp olive oil
- 4 chicken portions, about 150 g/5½ oz each, skinned if preferred
- 1 onion, chopped
- 2 celery sticks, roughly chopped
- 1½ tbsp plain flour
- 300 ml/10 fl oz clear apple juice
- 150 ml/5 fl oz chicken stock
- 1 cooking apple, cored and quartered
- 2 bay leaves
- 1–2 tsp honey
- 1 yellow pepper, deseeded and cut into chunks
- 1 large or 2 medium eating apples, cored and sliced
- 15 g/½ oz butter, melted
- 2 tbsp demerara sugar
- salt and pepper
- 1 tbsp chopped fresh mint, to garnish

1 Preheat the oven to 190°C/375°F/Gas Mark 5.

2 Heat the oil in a deep frying pan and cook the chicken over a medium–high heat, turning frequently, for 10 minutes, or until browned all over. Using a slotted spoon, transfer to a casserole.

3 Add the onion and celery to the frying pan and cook over a medium heat, stirring frequently, for 5 minutes, or until softened. Sprinkle in the flour and cook, stirring constantly, for 2 minutes, then remove from the heat. Gradually stir in the apple juice and stock, then return to the heat and bring to the boil, stirring. Add the cooking apple, bay leaves and honey. Season to taste with salt and pepper.

4 Pour over the chicken in the casserole, cover and cook in the preheated oven for 25 minutes. Add the yellow pepper and cook for a further 10–15 minutes, or until the chicken is tender and the juices run clear when a skewer is inserted into the thickest part of the meat.

5 Meanwhile, preheat the grill to high. Brush the eating apple slices with half the butter, sprinkle with half the sugar and cook under the grill for 2–3 minutes, or until the sugar has caramelized. Turn the slices over, brush with the remaining butter and sprinkle with the remaining sugar, then cook for a further 2 minutes. Serve the casserole immediately, garnished with the mint and caramelized apple slices.

one-pot chicken & rice

serves 4

- 30 g/1 oz butter
- 1 tbsp sunflower oil
- 4 large skinless, boneless chicken breasts
- 1 onion, chopped
- 1 garlic clove, crushed
- 2 red or green peppers, deseeded and finely chopped
- 55 g/2 oz sweetcorn kernels, drained if canned
- 55 g/2 oz peas
- 1 bay leaf, torn in half
- 200 ml/7 fl oz dry white wine
- 125 ml/4 fl oz quick-cook brown rice
- 250 ml/9 fl oz chicken stock
- salt and pepper
- chopped fresh parsley, to garnish

1 Melt the butter with the oil in a large flameproof casserole over a medium–high heat. Add the chicken breasts, in batches, if necessary, and fry for 3–5 minutes, until golden brown. Remove from the casserole and cook the remaining chicken breasts, then remove those from the casserole.

2 Pour off all but 1 tablespoon of the oil from the casserole. Add the onion, garlic and peppers and cook, stirring, for about 5 minutes, until soft but not brown. Return the chicken pieces to the casserole, add the sweetcorn, peas and bay leaf, then add the wine and bubble until it is almost all evaporated.

3 Scatter the rice over the chicken pieces, making sure it rests on top of the chicken, then pour in the stock and enough water to cover all the chicken pieces. Season to taste with salt and pepper.

4 Bring to the boil, cover and reduce the heat to very low. Cook for 20 minutes, until all the liquid has been absorbed, the rice is tender and the juices run clear when a skewer is inserted into the thickest part of the meat.

5 Taste and adjust the seasoning, adding salt and pepper if needed. Scatter over the parsley and serve immediately.

chicken casserole with a herb crust

serves 4
- 2 tbsp plain flour
- 4 whole chicken legs
- 1 tbsp olive oil
- 15 g/½ oz butter
- 1 onion, chopped
- 3 garlic cloves, sliced
- 4 parsnips, peeled and cut into large chunks
- 150 ml/5 fl oz dry white wine
- 850 ml/1½ pints chicken stock
- 3 leeks, white parts only, sliced
- 75 g/2¾ oz prunes, halved (optional)
- 1 tbsp English mustard
- bouquet garni
- 100 g/4 oz fresh breadcrumbs
- 75 g/2¾ oz Caerphilly cheese, crumbled
- 50 g/1¾ oz mixed fresh chopped tarragon and flat-leaf parsley
- salt and pepper

1 Preheat the oven to 180°C/350°F/Gas Mark 4.

2 Season the flour with salt and pepper to taste and toss the chicken in it to coat. Shake off any excess.

3 Heat the oil and butter in a flameproof casserole over a medium heat. Add the chicken and cook, turning frequently, until browned all over. Remove with a slotted spoon and keep warm.

4 Add the onion, garlic and parsnips to the casserole and cook for 20 minutes, or until the mixture is golden brown.

5 Add the wine, stock, leeks, prunes (if using), mustard and bouquet garni. Season to taste with salt and pepper. Return the chicken to the casserole, cover and cook in the preheated oven for 1 hour, or until the juices run clear when a skewer is inserted into the thickest part of the meat. Meanwhile mix together the breadcrumbs, cheese and herbs.

6 Remove the casserole from the oven and increase the temperature to 200°C/400°F/Gas Mark 6. Uncover the casserole and sprinkle over the breadcrumb mixture. Return to the oven for 10 minutes, uncovered, until the crust starts to brown slightly. Serve immediately.

chicken cobbler

serves 4
- 2 tbsp plain flour
- 4 skinless, boneless chicken breasts, cut into bite-sized chunks
- 25 g/1 oz butter
- 2 tbsp olive oil
- 1 large leek, trimmed and sliced
- 2 spring onions, trimmed and chopped
- 1 garlic clove, crushed
- 2 carrots, peeled and chopped
- 1 orange pepper, deseeded and chopped
- 1 tbsp tomato purée
- ½ tsp ground turmeric
- 200 ml/7 fl oz white wine
- 200 ml/7 fl oz chicken stock
- 1 bay leaf
- salt and pepper

cobbler topping
- 175 g/6 oz self-raising flour, plus extra for dusting
- 2 tsp baking powder
- ½ tsp ground turmeric
- pinch of salt
- 40 g/1½ oz butter
- 4–5 tbsp milk

1 Preheat the oven to 180°C/350°F/Gas Mark 4. Place the flour in a bowl with salt and pepper to taste. Toss the chicken in the seasoned flour until well coated and reserve any remaining flour.

2 Melt the butter with the oil in a large flameproof casserole, add the chicken and cook, stirring, until browned all over. Transfer the chicken to a plate and set aside.

3 Add the leek, spring onions and garlic to the casserole and cook over a medium heat, stirring, for 2 minutes, until softened. Add the carrots and orange pepper and cook for 2 minutes, then stir in the remaining seasoned flour, the tomato purée and turmeric. Pour in the wine and stock, bring to the boil, then reduce the heat and cook over a low heat, stirring, until thickened. Return the chicken to the pan and add the bay leaf. Cover and bake in the preheated oven for 30 minutes.

4 Meanwhile, sift the flour, baking powder, turmeric and salt into a mixing bowl. Rub in the butter until the mixture resembles fine breadcrumbs, then stir in enough of the milk to make a smooth dough. Transfer to a lightly floured work surface, knead lightly, then roll out to a thickness of about 1 cm/½ inch. Cut out rounds using a 5-cm/2-inch biscuit cutter.

5 Remove the casserole from the oven and discard the bay leaf. Arrange the dough rounds over the top, then return to the oven and bake for a further 30 minutes, or until the cobbler topping has risen and is lightly golden. Serve immediately.

potato, leek & chicken pie

serves 4

- 225 g/8 oz waxy potatoes, cubed
- 100 g/3½ oz butter
- 1 skinless, boneless chicken breast, about 175 g/6 oz, cubed
- 1 leek, sliced
- 150 g/5½ oz chestnut mushrooms, sliced
- 2½ tbsp plain flour
- 300 ml/10 fl oz milk
- 1 tbsp Dijon mustard
- 2 tbsp chopped fresh sage
- 225 g/8 oz filo pastry, thawed if frozen
- salt and pepper

1 Preheat the oven to 180°C/350°F/Gas Mark 4. Cook the potatoes in a saucepan of boiling water for 5 minutes. Drain and set aside.

2 Melt 60 g/2¼ oz of the butter in a frying pan and cook the chicken for 5 minutes, or until browned all over.

3 Add the leek and mushrooms and cook for 3 minutes, stirring. Stir in the flour and cook for 1 minute, stirring constantly. Gradually stir in the milk and bring to the boil. Add the mustard, sage and potatoes, season to taste with salt and pepper and simmer for 10 minutes.

4 Meanwhile, melt the remaining butter in a small saucepan. Line a deep pie dish with half of the sheets of filo pastry. Spoon the chicken mixture into the dish and cover with 1 sheet of pastry. Brush the pastry with a little of the melted butter and lay another sheet on top. Brush this sheet with butter.

5 Cut the remaining filo pastry into strips and fold them on top of the pie to create a ruffled effect. Brush the strips with the remaining melted butter and cook in the preheated oven for 45 minutes, or until golden brown and crisp. Serve immediately.

mexican turkey

serves 4
- 55 g/2 oz plain flour
- 4 turkey breast fillets
- 3 tbsp vegetable oil
- 1 onion, thinly sliced
- 1 red pepper, deseeded and sliced
- 300 ml/10 fl oz chicken stock
- 25 g/1 oz raisins
- 4 tomatoes, peeled, deseeded and chopped
- 1 tsp chilli powder
- ½ tsp ground cinnamon
- pinch of ground cumin
- 25 g/1 oz plain chocolate, finely chopped or grated
- salt and pepper
- fresh coriander sprigs, to garnish

1 Preheat the oven to 160°C/325°F/Gas Mark 3.

2 Spread the flour on a plate and season well with salt and pepper. Coat the turkey fillets in the seasoned flour, shaking off any excess. Reserve any remaining seasoned flour.

3 Heat the oil in a flameproof casserole. Add the turkey and cook over a medium heat, turning occasionally, for 5–10 minutes, or until browned all over. Transfer to a plate with a slotted spoon.

4 Add the onion and red pepper to the casserole. Cook over a low heat, stirring occasionally, for 5 minutes, or until softened. Sprinkle in the remaining seasoned flour and cook, stirring constantly, for 1 minute. Gradually stir in the stock, then add the raisins, tomatoes, chilli powder, cinnamon, cumin and chocolate. Season to taste with salt and pepper. Bring to the boil, stirring constantly.

5 Return the turkey to the casserole, cover and cook in the preheated oven for 50 minutes, until cooked through and the juices run clear when a skewer is inserted into the thickest part of the meat. Serve immediately, garnished with coriander sprigs

turkey in a piquant sauce

serves 4

- 2 tbsp plain flour
- 1 kg/2 lb 4 oz turkey pieces
- 25 g/1 oz butter
- 1 tbsp sunflower oil
- 2 onions, sliced
- 1 garlic clove, finely chopped
- 1 red pepper, deseeded and sliced
- 400 g/14 oz canned chopped tomatoes
- bouquet garni
- 150 ml/5 fl oz chicken stock
- salt and pepper
- 2 tbsp chopped fresh parsley, to garnish

1 Spread the flour on a plate and season well with salt and pepper. Coat the turkey in the seasoned flour, shaking off any excess. Reserve any remaining seasoned flour.

2 Melt the butter with the oil in a flameproof casserole or large saucepan. Add the turkey and cook over a medium heat, stirring, for 5–10 minutes, or until browned all over. Transfer the turkey pieces to a plate with a slotted spoon and keep warm.

3 Add the onions, garlic and red pepper to the casserole and cook, stirring occasionally, for 5 minutes, or until soft. Sprinkle in the remaining seasoned flour and cook, stirring constantly, for 1 minute.

4 Return the turkey to the casserole, then add the tomatoes, bouquet garni and stock. Bring to the boil, stirring constantly, then cover and simmer for 1¼ hours, or until the turkey is cooked through and tender.

5 Transfer the turkey to a serving platter with a slotted spoon. Discard the bouquet garni. Return the sauce to the boil and cook until reduced and thickened. Season to taste with salt and pepper and pour over the turkey. Serve immediately, garnished with parsley.

turkey with mole

serves 4

- 4 turkey portions, each cut into 4 pieces
- about 500 ml/18 fl oz chicken stock, plus extra for thinning
- about 250 ml/9 fl oz water
- 1 onion, chopped
- 1 whole garlic bulb, divided into cloves and peeled
- 1 celery stick, chopped
- 1 bay leaf
- 1 bunch fresh coriander, finely chopped
- 575 ml/19 fl oz mole sauce (use ready-made mole paste, thinned as instructed on the container)
- 4–5 tbsp sesame seeds

1 Preheat the oven to 190°C/375°F/Gas Mark 5.

2 Arrange the turkey in a large flameproof casserole. Pour the stock and water around the turkey, then add the onion, garlic, celery, bay leaf and half the coriander. Cover and bake in the preheated oven for 1–1½ hours, or until the turkey is very tender. Add extra liquid if needed.

3 Warm the mole sauce in a saucepan with enough stock to make it the consistency of thin cream.

4 Place the sesame seeds in an unoiled frying pan and dry-fry, shaking the pan, until lightly golden.

5 Arrange the turkey pieces on a serving plate and spoon the warmed mole sauce over the top. Sprinkle with the toasted sesame seeds and the remaining chopped coriander. Serve immediately.

italian turkey steaks

serves 4
- 1 tbsp olive oil
- 4 turkey escalopes or steaks
- 2 red peppers, deseeded and sliced
- 1 red onion, sliced
- 2 garlic cloves, finely chopped
- 300 ml/10 fl oz passata
- 150 ml/5 fl oz medium white wine
- 1 tbsp chopped fresh marjoram
- 400 g/14 oz canned cannellini beans, drained and rinsed
- 3 tbsp fresh white breadcrumbs
- salt and pepper
- fresh basil sprigs, to garnish

1 Heat the oil in a flameproof casserole, add the turkey and cook over a medium heat for 5–10 minutes, turning occasionally, until browned all over. Transfer to a plate using a slotted spoon.

2 Add the red peppers and onion to the casserole and cook over a low heat, stirring occasionally, for 5 minutes, or until softened. Add the garlic and cook for a further 2 minutes.

3 Return the turkey to the casserole and add the passata, wine and marjoram. Season to taste with salt and pepper. Bring to the boil, then reduce the heat, cover and simmer, stirring occasionally, for 25–30 minutes, or until the turkey is cooked through and tender. Meanwhile, preheat the grill to medium.

4 Stir the cannellini beans into the casserole and simmer for a further 5 minutes. Sprinkle the breadcrumbs over the top and place under the preheated grill for 2–3 minutes, or until golden. Serve immediately, garnished with basil sprigs.

duck in spiced orange sauce

serves 6

- 1 tbsp vegetable oil
- 6 duck legs, 175-225 g/6-8 oz each, all visible fat removed
- 2 lemon grass stalks
- 8 large garlic cloves, crushed
- 55 g/2 oz fresh ginger, thinly sliced
- 6 spring onions, 4 trimmed and crushed, 2 trimmed and thinly sliced diagonally
- 1 litre/1¾ pints orange juice
- juice of 2 limes
- 50 ml/2 fl oz Thai fish sauce
- 1 tbsp palm or granulated sugar
- 1 tsp five-spice powder
- 6 star anise
- 4 fresh red bird's eye chillies or dried red Chinese chillies
- 500-700 ml/18-24 fl oz water
- salt and pepper
- cooked rice and lime wedges, to serve

1 Heat the oil in a large saucepan over a high heat, then add the duck legs and cook for 20 minutes, cooking the first side until crisp and lifting off the base of the pan easily, then turning over and cooking the other side.

2 Meanwhile, discard the bruised leaves and root ends of the lemon grass stalks, then halve and crush 15–20 cm/6–8 inches of the lower stalks.

3 Transfer the duck legs to a plate using a slotted spoon. Drain off most of the fat from the saucepan, leaving about 1 tablespoon in the pan. Heat over a high heat, then add the garlic, ginger and crushed spring onions and stir-fry for 5 minutes, or until fragrant and golden. Add the orange juice, lime juice, fish sauce, sugar, five-spice powder, lemon grass, star anise and chillies.

4 Reduce the heat to low–medium and return the duck legs to the saucepan. Add enough of the water to cover by about 2.5 cm/1 inch. Simmer, partially covered, for 3–4 hours, or until the meat is tender and falling off the bones.

5 Adjust the seasoning, adding salt and pepper if needed. Remove the fat that has risen to the surface with a spoon. Garnish with the sliced spring onions and serve with rice and lime wedges.

duck legs with olives

serves 4

- 4 duck legs, all visible fat removed
- 800 g/1 lb 12 oz canned chopped tomatoes
- 8 garlic cloves, peeled but left whole
- 1 large onion, chopped
- 1 carrot, finely chopped
- 1 celery stick, finely chopped
- 3 fresh thyme sprigs
- 100 g/3½ oz Spanish green olives in brine, stuffed with pimientos, garlic or almonds, drained and rinsed
- 1 tsp finely grated orange rind
- salt and pepper

1 Put the duck legs in a flameproof casserole or a large heavy-based frying pan with a tight-fitting lid. Add the tomatoes, garlic, onion, carrot, celery, thyme and olives and stir together. Season to taste with salt and pepper.

2 Turn the heat to high and cook, uncovered, until the ingredients begin to bubble. Reduce the heat to low, cover tightly and simmer for 1¼–1½ hours, until the duck is very tender. Check occasionally and add a little water if the mixture appears to be drying out.

3 When the duck is tender, transfer to a serving platter with a slotted spoon, cover and keep warm. Leave the casserole uncovered, increase the heat to medium and cook, stirring, for about 10 minutes, until the mixture forms a sauce. Stir in the orange rind, then adjust the seasoning, adding salt and pepper if needed.

4 Mash the tender garlic cloves with a fork and spread over the duck legs. Spoon the sauce over the top. Serve immediately.

duck & red wine casserole

serves 4

- 4 duck portions, about 150 g/5½ oz each, all visible fat removed
- 2 tbsp olive oil
- 1 red onion, cut into wedges
- 2–3 garlic cloves, chopped
- 1 large carrot, chopped
- 2 celery sticks, chopped
- 2 tbsp plain flour
- 300 ml/10 fl oz full-bodied red wine
- 2 tbsp brandy (optional)
- 150–200 ml/5–7 fl oz chicken stock or water
- 7.5-cm/3-inch strip of orange rind
- 2 tsp redcurrant jelly
- 115 g/4 oz sugar snap peas
- 115 g/4 oz button mushrooms
- salt and pepper
- 1 tbsp chopped fresh parsley, to garnish

1 Heat a large frying pan for 1 minute, until warm but not piping hot. Put the duck portions in the frying pan and heat gently until the fat starts to run. Increase the heat a little, then cook, turning over halfway through, for 5 minutes, or until browned on both sides. Transfer to a flameproof casserole.

2 Add 1 tablespoon of the oil to the pan and cook the onion, garlic, carrot and celery, stirring frequently, for 5 minutes, or until softened. Sprinkle in the flour and cook, stirring constantly, for 2 minutes, then remove the pan from the heat.

3 Gradually stir in the wine, brandy, if using, and stock, then return to the heat and bring to the boil, stirring. Season to taste with salt and pepper, then add the orange rind and redcurrant jelly. Pour over the duck portions in the casserole, cover and simmer, stirring occasionally, for 1–1¼ hours.

4 Cook the sugar snap peas in a saucepan of boiling water for 3 minutes, then drain and add to the stew. Meanwhile, heat the remaining oil in a small saucepan and cook the mushrooms, stirring frequently, for 3 minutes, or until beginning to soften. Add to the casserole. Cook the stew for a further 5 minutes, or until the duck is tender. Serve immediately, garnished with the parsley.

duck jambalaya-style stew

serves 4

- 4 duck breasts, about 150 g/5½ oz each
- 2 tbsp olive oil
- 225 g/8 oz gammon, cut into small chunks
- 225 g/8 oz chorizo, outer casing removed
- 1 onion, chopped
- 3 garlic cloves, chopped
- 3 celery sticks, chopped
- 1–2 fresh red chillies, deseeded and chopped
- 1 green pepper, deseeded and chopped
- 600 ml/1 pint chicken stock
- 1 tbsp chopped fresh oregano
- 400 g/14 oz canned chopped tomatoes
- 1–2 tsp hot pepper sauce, or to taste
- fresh flat-leaf parsley sprigs, to garnish
- green salad and cooked rice, to serve

1 Remove and discard the skin and any fat from the duck breasts. Cut the flesh into bite-sized pieces.

2 Heat half the oil in a large deep frying pan and cook the duck, gammon and chorizo over a high heat, stirring frequently, for 5 minutes, or until browned all over. Using a slotted spoon, remove from the frying pan and set aside.

3 Add the onion, garlic, celery and chilli to the frying pan and cook over a medium heat, stirring frequently, for 5 minutes, or until softened. Add the green pepper, then stir in the stock, oregano, tomatoes and hot pepper sauce.

4 Bring to the boil, then reduce the heat and return the duck, gammon and chorizo to the frying pan. Cover and simmer, stirring occasionally, for 20 minutes, or until the duck and gammon are tender.

5 Serve immediately, garnished with parsley sprigs and accompanied by a green salad and rice.

braised asian duck

serves 4

- 3 tbsp soy sauce
- ½ tsp five-spice powder
- 4 duck legs or breasts, cut into pieces
- 3 tbsp vegetable oil
- 1 tsp toasted sesame oil
- 1 tsp finely chopped fresh ginger
- 1 large garlic clove, finely chopped
- 4 spring onions, white parts thickly sliced, green part shredded
- 2 tbsp rice wine or dry sherry
- 1 tbsp oyster sauce
- 3 whole star anise
- 2 tsp black peppercorns
- 450–600 ml/16 fl oz–1 pint chicken stock or water
- 2 tbsp cornflour
- salt and pepper

1 Combine 1 tablespoon of the soy sauce and the five-spice powder with salt and pepper to taste and rub over the duck pieces. Heat 2½ tablespoons of the vegetable oil in a large casserole. Add the duck and cook, turning occasionally, until browned all over. Remove the duck from the casserole with a slotted spoon and transfer to a plate.

2 Drain the fat from the casserole and wipe out with kitchen paper. Heat the sesame oil and the remaining vegetable oil. Add the ginger and garlic. Cook for a few seconds. Add the sliced white spring onion and cook for a few seconds.

3 Return the duck to the casserole. Add the rice wine, oyster sauce, star anise, peppercorns and the remaining soy sauce. Pour in enough stock to just cover. Bring to the boil, cover and simmer gently for 1½ hours, adding more water if needed.

4 Mix the cornflour with 2 tablespoons of the cooking liquid to a smooth paste. Add to the casserole, stirring until the sauce has thickened. Garnish with the shredded green spring onion and serve immediately.

Mmmm...
fish &
seafood

bouillabaisse

serves 8

- 1.25 kg/2 lb 12 oz sea bass, filleted, skinned and cut into bite-sized chunks
- 1.25 kg/2 lb 12 oz red snapper, filleted, skinned and cut into bite-sized chunks
- 3 tbsp extra virgin olive oil
- grated rind of 1 orange
- 1 garlic clove, finely chopped
- pinch of saffron threads
- 2 tbsp pastis, such as Pernod
- 450 g/1 lb live mussels
- 1 large cooked crab
- 1 small fennel bulb, finely chopped
- 2 celery sticks, finely chopped
- 1 onion, finely chopped
- 1.2 litres/2 pints fish stock
- 225 g/8 oz small new potatoes, scrubbed
- 225 g/8 oz tomatoes, peeled, deseeded and chopped
- 450 g/1 lb large raw prawns, peeled and deveined
- salt and pepper

1 Put the fish chunks in a large bowl and add 2 tablespoons of the oil, the orange rind, garlic, saffron and pastis. Toss the fish pieces until well coated, cover and leave to marinate in the refrigerator for 30 minutes.

2 Meanwhile, clean the mussels by scrubbing or scraping the shells and pulling off any beards. Discard any with broken shells and any that refuse to close when tapped. Remove the meat from the crab, chop and reserve.

3 Heat the remaining oil in a large flameproof casserole and cook the fennel, celery and onion over a low heat, stirring occasionally, for 5 minutes, or until softened. Add the stock and bring to the boil. Add the potatoes and tomatoes and cook over a medium heat for 7 minutes.

4 Reduce the heat and add the fish to the stew, beginning with the thickest pieces, then add the mussels, prawns and crab and simmer until the fish is opaque, the mussels have opened and the prawns have turned pink. Discard any mussels that remain closed. Season to taste with salt and pepper and serve immediately.

seafood chilli

serves 4

- 115 g/4 oz raw prawns, peeled and deveined
- 250 g/9 oz prepared scallops, thawed if frozen
- 115 g/4 oz monkfish fillet, cut into chunks
- 1 lime, peeled and thinly sliced
- 1 tbsp chilli powder
- 1 tsp ground cumin
- 3 tbsp chopped fresh coriander
- 2 garlic cloves, finely chopped
- 1 fresh green chilli, deseeded and chopped
- 2–3 tbsp vegetable oil
- 1 onion, roughly chopped
- 1 red pepper, deseeded and roughly chopped
- 1 yellow pepper, deseeded and roughly chopped
- ¼ tsp ground cloves
- pinch of ground cinnamon
- pinch of cayenne pepper
- 350 ml/12 fl oz fish stock
- 400 g/14 oz canned chopped tomatoes
- 400 g/14 oz canned red kidney beans, drained and rinsed
- salt

1 Place the prawns, scallops, monkfish and lime slices in a large non-metallic dish with ¼ teaspoon of the chilli powder, ¼ teaspoon of the ground cumin, 1 tablespoon of the coriander, half the garlic, the chilli and 1 tablespoon of the oil. Cover with clingfilm and leave to marinate for up to 1 hour.

2 Meanwhile, heat 1 tablespoon of the remaining oil in a flameproof casserole or large heavy-based saucepan. Add the onion, the remaining garlic and the red and yellow peppers and cook over a low heat, stirring occasionally, for 5 minutes, or until softened. Add the remaining chilli powder, the remaining cumin, the cloves, cinnamon and cayenne pepper with the remaining oil, if necessary, and season to taste with salt. Cook, stirring, for 5 minutes, then gradually stir in the stock and tomatoes. Partially cover and simmer for 25 minutes.

3 Add the beans to the casserole and spoon the fish and shellfish on top. Cover and cook for 10 minutes, or until the fish and shellfish are cooked through. Sprinkle with the remaining coriander and serve immediately.

fisherman's stew

serves 6

- 1.5 kg/3 lb 5 oz live mussels
- 3 tbsp olive oil
- 2 onions, chopped
- 3 garlic cloves, finely chopped
- 1 red pepper, deseeded and sliced
- 3 carrots, chopped
- 800 g/1 lb 12 oz canned chopped tomatoes
- 125 ml/4 fl oz dry white wine
- 2 tbsp tomato purée
- 1 tbsp chopped fresh dill
- 2 tbsp chopped fresh parsley
- 1 tbsp chopped fresh thyme
- 1 tbsp torn fresh basil leaves, plus extra leaves to garnish
- 900 g/2 lb white fish fillets, cut into chunks
- 450 g/1 lb raw prawns, peeled and deveined
- 350 ml/12 fl oz fish stock or water
- salt and pepper

1 Clean the mussels by scrubbing or scraping the shells and pulling off any beards. Discard any with broken shells and any that refuse to close when tapped. Rinse the mussels under cold running water.

2 Heat the oil in a flameproof casserole. Add the onions, garlic, red pepper and carrots and cook over a low heat, stirring occasionally, for 5 minutes, or until softened.

3 Add the tomatoes, wine, tomato purée and herbs. Bring to the boil, then reduce the heat and simmer for 20 minutes.

4 Add the fish, mussels, prawns and stock with salt and pepper to taste. Return the stew to the boil and simmer for 6–8 minutes, or until the prawns have turned pink and the mussels have opened. Discard any mussels that remain closed.

5 Serve immediately, garnished with basil leaves.

mediterranean fish casserole

serves 6

- 2 tbsp olive oil
- 1 red onion, peeled and sliced
- 2 garlic cloves, peeled and chopped
- 2 red peppers, deseeded and thinly sliced
- 400 g/14 oz canned chopped tomatoes
- 1 tsp chopped fresh oregano or marjoram
- a few saffron strands, soaked in 1 tbsp warm water for 2 minutes
- 450 g/1 lb white fish fillets, cut into chunks
- 450 g/1 lb prepared squid, cut into rings
- 300 ml/10 fl oz fish or vegetable stock
- 115 g/4 oz cooked peeled prawns, plus extra in their shells to garnish
- salt and pepper
- 2 tbsp chopped fresh parsley, to garnish
- crusty bread, to serve

1 Heat the oil in a frying pan and fry the onion and garlic over a medium heat for 2–3 minutes, until beginning to soften.

2 Add the red peppers to the pan and continue to cook over a low heat for a further 5 minutes. Add the tomatoes, oregano and saffron and stir well.

3 Preheat the oven to 200°C/400°F/Gas Mark 6.

4 Place the fish in a large casserole with the squid. Pour in the vegetable mixture and the stock, stir well and season to taste with salt and pepper.

5 Cover and cook in the preheated oven for about 30 minutes, until the fish is tender and cooked through. Add the prawns and heat through.

6 Spoon into warmed bowls and garnish with the whole prawns and the parsley. Serve immediately with crusty bread to mop up the casserole juices.

spanish fish in tomato sauce

serves 4
- 4 tbsp lemon juice
- 6 tbsp olive oil
- 4 swordfish steaks, about 175 g/6 oz each
- 1 onion, finely chopped
- 1 garlic clove, finely chopped
- 1 tbsp plain flour
- 225 g/8 oz tomatoes, peeled, deseeded and chopped
- 1 tbsp tomato purée
- 300 ml/10 fl oz dry white wine
- salt and pepper
- fresh dill sprigs, to garnish

1 Preheat the oven to 180°C/350°F/Gas Mark 4.

2 Place the lemon juice and 4 tablespoons of the oil in a shallow non-metallic dish, stir well and season to taste with salt and pepper. Add the swordfish steaks, turning to coat thoroughly, then cover with clingfilm and leave to marinate in the refrigerator for 1 hour.

3 Heat the remaining oil in a flameproof casserole. Add the onion and cook over a low heat, stirring occasionally, for 10 minutes, or until golden. Add the garlic and cook, stirring frequently, for 2 minutes. Sprinkle in the flour and cook, stirring, for 1 minute, then add the tomatoes, tomato purée and wine. Bring to the boil, stirring.

4 Add the fish to the casserole, pushing it down under the liquid. Cover and cook in the preheated oven for 20 minutes, or until cooked through and the swordfish flakes easily. Serve immediately, garnished with dill sprigs.

monkfish ragoût

serves 4–6

- 2 tbsp olive oil
- 1 small onion, finely chopped
- 1 red pepper, deseeded and cut into 2.5-cm/1-inch pieces
- 115 g/4 oz mushrooms, finely sliced
- 3 garlic cloves, very finely chopped
- 1 tbsp tomato purée
- 2 tbsp chopped fresh flat-leaf parsley
- ½ tsp dried oregano
- 400 g/14 oz canned chopped tomatoes
- 150 ml/5 fl oz dry red wine
- 550 g/1 lb 4 oz monkfish, skinned and cubed
- 1 courgette, sliced
- salt and pepper
- 6–8 fresh basil leaves, shredded, to garnish
- crusty bread, to serve

1 Heat the oil in a heavy-based saucepan or flameproof casserole over a medium heat. Add the onion, red pepper and mushrooms and cook for 5 minutes, or until beginning to soften.

2 Stir in the garlic, tomato purée, parsley and oregano. Cook for 1 minute. Pour in the tomatoes and wine. Season to taste with salt and pepper. Bring to the boil, then simmer gently for 10–15 minutes, or until slightly thickened.

3 Add the monkfish and courgette. Cover and simmer for 15 minutes, or until the monkfish is cooked and the courgette is tender but still brightly coloured.

4 Garnish with the basil and serve immediately with crusty bread.

seafood stew

serves 4

- 1 yellow pepper, deseeded and quartered
- 1 red pepper, deseeded and quartered
- 1 orange pepper, deseeded and quartered
- 450 g/1 lb ripe tomatoes
- 2 large fresh green chillies, such as poblano
- 6 garlic cloves, peeled but kept whole
- 2 tsp dried oregano or dried mixed herbs
- 2 tbsp olive oil, plus extra for drizzling
- 1 large onion, finely chopped
- 450 ml/16 fl oz fish, vegetable or chicken stock
- finely grated rind and juice of 1 lime
- 2 tbsp chopped fresh coriander, plus extra to garnish
- 1 bay leaf
- 450 g/1 lb red snapper fillets, skinned and cut into chunks
- 225 g/8 oz raw prawns, peeled and deveined
- 225 g/8 oz raw squid rings
- salt and pepper
- warmed flour tortillas, to serve

1 Preheat the oven to 200°C/400°F/Gas Mark 6.

2 Put the pepper quarters, skin-side up, in a roasting tin with the tomatoes, chillies and garlic. Sprinkle with the oregano and drizzle with oil. Roast in the preheated oven for 30 minutes, or until the peppers are well browned and softened.

3 Remove the roasted vegetables from the oven and leave to stand until cool enough to handle. Peel off the skins from the peppers, tomatoes and chillies and chop the flesh. Finely chop the garlic.

4 Heat the oil in a large saucepan and cook the onion, stirring frequently, for 5 minutes, or until softened. Add the peppers, tomatoes, chillies, garlic, stock, lime rind and juice, coriander and bay leaf with salt and pepper to taste. Bring to the boil, then stir in the seafood. Reduce the heat, cover and simmer gently for 10 minutes, or until the fish and squid are just cooked through and the prawns have turned pink.

5 Discard the bay leaf, then garnish with coriander and serve immediately with flour tortillas.

paella del mar

serves 6

- 450 g/1 lb live mussels
- 6 squid
- 125 ml/4 fl oz olive oil
- 1 onion, chopped
- 2 garlic cloves,
  finely chopped
- 1 red pepper, deseeded
  and cut into strips
- 1 green pepper, deseeded
  and cut into strips
- 400 g/14 oz risotto rice
- 2 tomatoes, peeled and
  chopped
- 1 tbsp tomato purée
- 175 g/6 oz monkfish fillet,
  cut into chunks
- 175 g/6 oz red mullet fillet,
  cut into chunks
- 175 g/6 oz cod fillet, cut into
  chunks
- 500 ml/18 fl oz fish stock
- 115 g/4 oz fresh or frozen
  green beans, halved
- 115 g/4 oz fresh or frozen
  peas
- 6 canned artichoke hearts,
  drained
- ¼ tsp saffron threads
- 12 raw Mediterranean or
  tiger prawns
- salt and pepper

1 Clean the mussels by scrubbing or scraping the shells and pulling off any beards. Discard any with broken shells and any that refuse to close when tapped. Rinse the mussels under cold running water.

2 To prepare each squid, hold the body firmly and grasp the tentacles just inside the body. Pull firmly to remove the innards. Find the transparent quill and remove. Grasp the wings on the outside of the body and pull to remove the outer skin. Trim the tentacles just below the beak and reserve. Wash the body and tentacles under running water. Slice the body into rings. Drain well on kitchen paper.

3 Heat the oil in a paella pan or flameproof casserole. Add the onion, garlic and peppers and cook over a medium heat, stirring, for 5 minutes, or until softened. Stir in the prepared squid and cook for 2 minutes. Add the rice and cook, stirring, until transparent and coated with oil.

4 Add the tomatoes, tomato purée and fish and cook for 3 minutes, then add the stock. Gently stir in the beans, peas, artichoke hearts and saffron and season to taste with salt and pepper.

5 Arrange the mussels around the edge of the pan and top the mixture with the prawns. Bring to the boil, reduce the heat and simmer, shaking the pan from time to time, for 15–20 minutes, or until the rice is tender. Discard any mussels that remain closed. Serve immediately.

squid stew

serves 4

- 750 g/1 lb 10 oz squid
- 3 tbsp olive oil
- 1 onion, chopped
- 3 garlic cloves,
  finely chopped
- 1 tsp chopped fresh thyme
  leaves
- 400 g/14 oz canned
  chopped tomatoes
- 150 ml/5 fl oz red wine
- 300 ml/10 fl oz water
- 1 tbsp chopped
  fresh parsley
- salt and pepper
- crusty bread, to serve

1 Preheat the oven to 140°C/275°F/Gas Mark 1.

2 To prepare each squid, hold the body firmly and grasp the tentacles just inside the body. Pull firmly to remove the innards. Find the transparent quill and remove. Grasp the wings on the outside of the body and pull to remove the outer skin. Trim the tentacles just below the beak and reserve. Wash the body and tentacles under running water. Slice the body into rings. Drain well on kitchen paper.

3 Heat the oil in a large flameproof casserole. Add the prepared squid and cook over a medium heat, stirring occasionally, until lightly browned.

4 Reduce the heat and add the onion, garlic and thyme. Cook, stirring occasionally, for a further 5 minutes, until softened.

5 Stir in the tomatoes, wine and water. Bring to the boil, then transfer the casserole to the preheated oven for 2 hours. Stir in the parsley and season to taste with salt and pepper. Serve immediately with crusty bread.

seafood in saffron sauce

serves 4

- 225 g/8 oz live mussels
- 225 g/8 oz live clams
- 2 tbsp olive oil
- 1 onion, sliced
- pinch of saffron threads
- 1 tbsp chopped fresh thyme
- 2 garlic cloves, finely chopped
- 800 g/1 lb 12 oz canned tomatoes, drained and chopped
- 175 ml/6 fl oz dry white wine
- 2 litres/3½ pints fish stock
- 350 g/12 oz red mullet fillets, cut into bite-sized chunks
- 450 g/1 lb monkfish fillets, cut into bite-sized chunks
- 225 g/8 oz raw squid rings
- 2 tbsp fresh shredded basil leaves
- salt and pepper
- crusty bread, to serve

1 Clean the mussels and clams by scrubbing or scraping the shells and pulling off any beards that are attached to the mussels. Discard any with broken shells and any that refuse to close when tapped.

2 Heat the oil in a large flameproof casserole and cook the onion with the saffron and thyme over a low heat, stirring occasionally, for 5 minutes, or until softened. Add the garlic and cook, stirring, for 2 minutes.

3 Add the tomatoes, wine and stock, season to taste with salt and pepper and stir well. Bring to the boil, then reduce the heat and simmer for 15 minutes.

4 Add the fish chunks and simmer for a further 3 minutes. Add the clams, mussels and squid rings and simmer for a further 5 minutes, or until the mussels and clams have opened. Discard any that remain closed. Stir in the basil and serve immediately, accompanied by plenty of crusty bread to mop up the juices.

louisiana gumbo

serves 6

- 2 tbsp sunflower
  or vegetable oil
- 175 g/6 oz okra, trimmed
  and cut into 2.5-cm/1-inch
  pieces
- 2 onions, finely chopped
- 4 celery sticks, very finely
  chopped
- 1 garlic clove,
  finely chopped
- 2 tbsp plain flour
- ½ tsp caster sugar
- 1 tsp ground cumin
- 700 ml/1¼ pints fish stock
- 1 red pepper, deseeded
  and chopped
- 1 green pepper, deseeded
  and chopped
- 2 large tomatoes, chopped
- 4 tbsp chopped
  fresh parsley
- 1 tbsp chopped
  fresh coriander
- dash of Tabasco sauce
- 350 g/12 oz cod or haddock
  fillets, skinned and cut into
  2.5-cm/1-inch chunks
- 350 g/12 oz monkfish fillets,
  skinned and cut into
  2.5-cm/1-inch chunks
- 350 g/12 oz large raw
  prawns, peeled and
  deveined
- salt and pepper

1 Heat half the oil in a large flameproof casserole or a large saucepan with a tight-fitting lid and cook the okra over a low heat, stirring frequently, for 5 minutes, or until browned. Using a slotted spoon, remove from the casserole and set aside.

2 Heat the remaining oil in the casserole and cook the onion and celery over a medium heat, stirring frequently, for 5 minutes, or until softened. Add the garlic and cook, stirring, for 1 minute. Sprinkle in the flour, sugar and cumin with salt and pepper to taste. Cook, stirring constantly, for 2 minutes, then remove from the heat.

3 Gradually stir in the stock, then return to the heat and bring to the boil, stirring. Return the okra to the casserole and add the peppers and tomatoes. Partially cover, reduce the heat to very low and simmer gently, stirring occasionally, for 10 minutes.

4 Add the herbs and Tabasco sauce to taste. Gently stir in the fish and prawns. Cover and simmer gently for 5 minutes, or until the fish is cooked through and the prawns have turned pink. Transfer to a warmed serving dish and serve immediately.

catfish stew

serves 4

- 2 tsp garlic granules
- 1 tsp celery salt
- 1 tsp pepper
- 1 tsp curry powder
- 1 tsp paprika
- pinch of caster sugar
- 4–8 slices catfish or rockfish, about 900 g/2 lb total weight
- 2 tbsp red wine vinegar
- 40 g/1½ oz plain flour
- 6 tbsp sunflower oil
- 1 onion, finely chopped
- 2 garlic cloves, finely chopped
- 280 g/10 oz tomatoes, peeled and chopped
- 1 fresh marjoram sprig
- 600 ml/1 pint fish stock
- ¼ tsp ground cumin
- ¼ tsp ground cinnamon
- 2 fresh red or green chillies, deseeded and finely chopped
- 1 red pepper, deseeded and finely chopped
- 1 yellow pepper, deseeded and finely chopped
- salt
- fresh flat-leaf parsley sprigs, to garnish
- crusty bread, to serve

1 Mix together the garlic granules, celery salt, pepper, curry powder, paprika and sugar in a small bowl. Place the fish in a non-metallic dish and sprinkle with half the spice mixture. Turn the fish over and sprinkle with the remaining spice mixture. Add the vinegar and turn to coat. Cover with clingfilm and set aside in a cool place to marinate for 1 hour.

2 Spread out the flour in a shallow dish. Drain the fish and dip into the flour to coat, shaking off any excess.

3 Heat 4 tablespoons of the oil in a frying pan. Add the fish and cook over a medium heat for 2–3 minutes on each side. Remove with a fish slice and set aside.

4 Wipe out the frying pan with kitchen paper, add the remaining oil and heat. Add the onion and cook over a low heat, stirring occasionally, for 5 minutes, until soft. Add the garlic and cook, stirring, for a further 2 minutes. Add the tomatoes and marjoram, increase the heat to medium and cook, stirring occasionally, for 8 minutes.

5 Stir in the stock, cumin and cinnamon and add the fish, chillies and peppers. Bring to the boil, then reduce the heat and simmer for 8–10 minutes, until the fish flakes easily and the sauce has thickened. Season to taste with salt and garnish with parsley sprigs. Serve immediately with crusty bread.

french fish stew

serves 4–6

- large pinch of saffron threads
- 2 tbsp olive oil
- 1 large onion, finely chopped
- 1 fennel bulb, thinly sliced, green fronds reserved
- 2 large garlic cloves, crushed
- 4 tbsp pastis
- 1 litre/1¾ pints fish stock
- 2 large ripe tomatoes, peeled, deseeded and diced
- 1 tbsp tomato purée
- 1 bay leaf
- pinch of sugar
- pinch of dried chilli flakes (optional)
- 25 large raw prawns, peeled and deveined
- 1 prepared squid, cut into rings
- 900 g/2 lb Mediterranean fish fillets, such as sea bass, monkfish or red snapper, cut into large chunks
- salt and pepper

1 Put the saffron threads in a small unoiled frying pan over a high heat and toast, stirring constantly, for 1 minute. Immediately tip the saffron threads out of the pan and set aside.

2 Heat the oil in a large flameproof casserole over a medium heat. Add the onion and fennel and sauté for 3 minutes, then add the garlic and continue sautéeing for a further 5 minutes, or until the onion and fennel are soft but not coloured.

3 Remove the casserole from the heat. Warm the pastis in a small saucepan, ignite and pour it over the onion and fennel to flambé. When the flames have died down, return the casserole to the heat and stir in the stock, tomatoes, tomato purée, bay leaf, sugar, chilli flakes, if using, and salt and pepper to taste. Slowly bring to the boil, then reduce the heat to low and simmer, uncovered, for 15 minutes.

4 Add the prawns and squid and simmer until the prawns turn pink and the squid is opaque. Do not overcook. Transfer the prawns and squid to serving bowls and keep warm.

5 Add the fish and the reserved saffron to the casserole and simmer for 5 minutes, or until the flesh flakes easily. Transfer the fish and broth to the bowls with the prawns and squid and garnish with the fennel fronds. Serve immediately.

moroccan fish tagine

serves 4

- 2 tbsp olive oil
- 1 large onion, finely chopped
- pinch of saffron threads
- ½ tsp ground cinnamon
- 1 tsp ground coriander
- ½ tsp ground cumin
- ½ tsp ground turmeric
- 200 g/7 oz canned chopped tomatoes
- 300 ml/10 fl oz fish stock
- 4 small red mullet, cleaned, boned and heads and tails removed
- 55 g/2 oz stoned green olives
- 1 tbsp chopped preserved lemon
- 3 tbsp chopped fresh coriander
- salt and pepper

1 Heat the oil in a flameproof casserole. Add the onion and cook gently over a very low heat, stirring occasionally, for 10 minutes, or until softened but not coloured. Add the saffron, cinnamon, ground coriander, cumin and turmeric and cook for a further 30 seconds, stirring constantly.

2 Add the tomatoes and stock and stir well. Bring to the boil, reduce the heat, cover and simmer for 15 minutes. Uncover and simmer for 20–35 minutes, or until thickened.

3 Cut each red mullet in half, then add the fish pieces to the casserole, pushing them down under the liquid. Simmer the stew for a further 5–6 minutes, or until the fish is just cooked.

4 Carefully stir in the olives, preserved lemon and chopped coriander. Season to taste with salt and pepper and serve immediately.

seafood hotpot with red wine

serves 4–6

- 350 g/12 oz live mussels, scrubbed and debearded
- 4 tbsp olive oil
- 1 onion, finely chopped
- 1 green pepper, deseeded and chopped
- 2 garlic cloves, very finely chopped
- 5 tbsp tomato purée
- 1 tbsp chopped fresh flat-leaf parsley
- 1 tsp dried oregano
- 400 g/14 oz canned chopped tomatoes
- 225 ml/8 fl oz dry red wine
- 450 g/1 lb firm white fish, such as cod or monkfish, cut into 5-cm/2-inch pieces
- 115 g/4 oz prepared scallops, halved
- 115 g/4 oz raw prawns, peeled and deveined
- 200 g/7 oz canned crabmeat, drained
- 10–15 fresh basil leaves, shredded
- salt and pepper

1 Discard any mussels with broken shells and any that refuse to close when tapped.

2 Heat the oil in a heavy-based saucepan or flameproof casserole over a medium heat. Add the onion and green pepper and cook for 5 minutes, or until beginning to soften.

3 Stir in the garlic, tomato purée, parsley and oregano and cook for 1 minute, stirring.

4 Pour in the tomatoes and wine. Season to taste with salt and pepper.

5 Bring to the boil, then cover and simmer over a low heat for 30 minutes. Add the fish, cover and simmer for 15 minutes.

6 Add the mussels, scallops, prawns and crabmeat. Cover and cook for a further 15 minutes. Discard any mussels that remain closed. Stir in the basil and serve immediately.

rustic fish stew

serves 4–6

- 4 tbsp olive oil
- 1 onion, chopped
- 2 celery sticks, sliced
- 3 garlic cloves, sliced
- 1 tbsp smoked paprika
- small pinch of saffron strands
- 150 ml/5 fl oz dry sherry
- 600 ml/1 pint chicken or fish stock
- 2 bay leaves
- 400 g/14 oz canned chopped tomatoes
- 550 g / 1 lb 4 oz waxy potatoes, peeled and cut into quarters
- 2 red peppers, deseeded and sliced
- 1.5 kg/3 lb 5 oz mixed seafood, cut into bite-sized pieces
- salt and pepper
- chopped fresh parsley and grated lemon rind, to garnish
- extra virgin olive oil, to serve

1 Heat the olive oil in a saucepan and fry the onion, celery and garlic over a medium heat for 2–3 minutes, until beginning to soften.

2 Add the paprika and saffron and cook for a further minute, then add the sherry and reduce by half.

3 Add the stock, bay leaves, tomatoes and potatoes, season to taste with salt and pepper and cook for 10 minutes, or until the potatoes are almost cooked. Add the red peppers and cook for an additional 10 minutes.

4 If using live mussels, clean them by scrubbing or scraping the shells and pulling off any beards. Discard any with broken shells and any that refuse to close when tapped. Rinse the mussels under cold running water.

5 Carefully add the mussels, if using, and seafood to the saucepan, stirring only once or twice. Cover and cook for 8–10 minutes, or until the seafood is cooked through. Discard any mussels that remain closed, turn off the heat and leave to stand for 2 minutes.

6 Serve the stew in a large bowl, garnished with parsley and lemon rind. Drizzle with extra virgin olive oil and serve immediately.

squid & prawns with broad beans

serves 4

- 2 tbsp olive oil
- 4 spring onions, thinly sliced
- 2 garlic cloves, finely chopped
- 500 g/1 lb 2 oz prepared squid, cut into rings
- 100 ml/3½ fl oz dry white wine
- 600 g/1 lb 5 oz fresh young broad beans in their pods, shelled to give about 225 g/8 oz, or 225 g/8 oz frozen baby broad beans
- 250 g/9 oz raw tiger prawns, peeled and deveined
- 4 tbsp chopped fresh flat-leaf parsley
- salt and pepper
- crusty bread, to serve

1 Heat the oil in a large frying pan with a lid or a flameproof casserole, add the spring onions and cook over a medium heat, stirring occasionally, for 4–5 minutes, until softened. Add the garlic and cook, stirring, for 30 seconds until softened. Add the squid and cook over a high heat, stirring occasionally, for 2 minutes, or until golden brown.

2 Add the wine and bring to the boil. Add the broad beans, then reduce the heat, cover and simmer for 5–8 minutes if using fresh beans or 4–5 minutes if using frozen beans, until the beans are tender.

3 Add the prawns and parsley, re-cover and simmer for a further 2–3 minutes, until the prawns have turned pink. Season to taste with salt and pepper. Serve immediately with crusty bread to mop up the juices.

mixed fish cobbler

serves 4
- 25 g/1 oz butter
- 2 large leeks, trimmed and sliced
- 150 g/5½ oz white mushrooms, sliced
- 2 courgettes, sliced
- 4 large tomatoes, peeled and chopped
- 1 tbsp chopped fresh dill
- 100 ml/3½ fl oz white wine
- 200 ml/7 fl oz fish stock
- 4 tsp cornflour
- 225 g/8 oz cod, cut into bite-sized chunks
- 225 g/8 oz haddock, cut into bite-sized chunks
- salt and pepper

cobbler topping
- 175 g/6 oz self-raising flour, plus extra for dusting
- 2 tsp baking powder
- pinch of salt
- 1 tbsp chopped fresh dill
- 40 g/1½ oz butter
- 4–5 tbsp milk

1 Preheat the oven to 200°C/400°F/Gas Mark 6.

2 Melt the butter in a large flameproof casserole over a low heat. Add the leeks and cook, stirring, for 2 minutes, until slightly softened. Add the mushrooms, courgettes, tomatoes and dill, and cook, stirring, for a further 3 minutes.

3 Stir in the wine and stock, bring to the boil, then reduce the heat to a simmer. Mix the cornflour with a little water to form a paste, then stir it into the casserole. Cook, stirring constantly, until thickened, then season to taste with salt and pepper and remove from the heat.

4 To make the cobbler topping, sift the flour, baking powder and salt into a large mixing bowl. Stir in the dill, then rub in the butter until the mixture resembles fine breadcrumbs. Stir in enough of the milk to make a smooth dough. Transfer to a lightly floured work surface, knead lightly, then roll out to a thickness of about 1 cm/½ inch. Cut out rounds using a 5-cm/2-inch biscuit cutter.

5 Add the cod and haddock to the casserole and stir gently to mix. Arrange the dough rounds over the top, then bake in the preheated oven for 30 minutes, or until the cobbler topping has risen and is lightly golden. Serve immediately.

fisherman's pie

serves 6
- 900 g/2 lb white fish fillets, such as plaice, skinned
- 150 ml/5 fl oz dry white wine
- 1 tbsp chopped fresh parsley, tarragon or dill
- 100 g/3½ oz butter, plus extra for greasing
- 175 g/6 oz small mushrooms, sliced
- 175 g/6 oz cooked peeled prawns
- 40 g/1½ oz plain flour
- 125 ml/4 fl oz double cream
- 900 g/2 lb floury potatoes, peeled and cut into chunks
- salt and pepper

1 Preheat the oven to 180°C/350°F/Gas Mark 4. Grease a 1.7-litre/3-pint baking dish.

2 Fold the fish fillets in half and put in the prepared dish. Season well with salt and pepper, pour over the wine and scatter over the parsley. Cover with foil and bake in the preheated oven for 15 minutes, until the fish starts to flake. Strain off the liquid and reserve for the sauce. Increase the oven temperature to 220°C/425°F/Gas Mark 7.

3 Melt 15 g/½ oz of the butter in a frying pan over a medium heat, add the mushrooms and cook, stirring frequently, for 5 minutes. Spoon over the fish. Scatter over the prawns.

4 Heat 55 g/2 oz of the remaining butter in a saucepan and stir in the flour. Cook for 3–4 minutes without browning, stirring constantly. Remove from the heat and gradually add the reserved cooking liquid, stirring well after each addition. Return to the heat and slowly bring to the boil, stirring constantly, until thickened. Add the cream and season to taste with salt and pepper. Pour over the fish in the dish and smooth over the surface.

5 Bring a large saucepan of lightly salted water to the boil, add the potatoes and cook for 15–20 minutes. Drain well and mash until smooth. Season to taste with salt and pepper, then add the remaining butter, stirring until melted. Pile or pipe the potato onto the fish and sauce and bake for 10–15 minutes, until golden brown. Serve immediately.

macaroni &
seafood bake

serves 4

- 350 g/12 oz dried macaroni
- 85 g/3 oz butter, plus extra for greasing
- 2 small fennel bulbs, trimmed and thinly sliced
- 175 g/6 oz mushrooms, thinly sliced
- 175 g/6 oz cooked peeled prawns
- pinch of cayenne pepper
- 600 ml/1 pint béchamel sauce (see page 9)
- 55 g/2 oz freshly grated Parmesan cheese
- 2 large tomatoes, halved and sliced
- olive oil, for brushing
- 1 tsp dried oregano
- salt

1 Preheat the oven to 180°C/350°F/Gas Mark 4. Grease a large ovenproof dish.

2 Bring a large saucepan of lightly salted water to the boil. Add the pasta, return to the boil and cook for 8–10 minutes, or until tender but still firm to the bite. Drain and return to the saucepan. Add 25 g/1 oz of the butter to the pasta, cover, shake the saucepan and keep warm.

3 Melt the remaining butter in a separate saucepan. Add the fennel and cook for 3–4 minutes. Stir in the mushrooms and cook for a further 2 minutes. Stir in the prawns, then remove the saucepan from the heat.

4 Stir the cooked pasta, cayenne pepper and prawn mixture into the béchamel sauce. Pour the mixture into the prepared dish and spread evenly. Sprinkle over the Parmesan and arrange the tomato slices around the edge. Brush the tomatoes with oil, then sprinkle over the oregano. Bake in the preheated oven for 25 minutes, or until golden brown. Serve immediately.

seafood lasagne

serves 4

- 50 g/1¾ oz butter, plus extra for greasing
- 50 g/1¾ oz plain flour
- 1 tsp mustard powder
- 600 ml/1 pint milk
- 2 tbsp olive oil
- 1 onion, chopped
- 2 garlic cloves, finely chopped
- 450 g/1 lb mixed mushrooms, sliced
- 150 ml/5 fl oz white wine
- 400 g/14 oz canned chopped tomatoes
- 450 g/1 lb skinless white fish fillets, cut into chunks
- 225 g/8 oz prepared scallops
- 4–6 sheets fresh lasagne
- 225 g/8 oz mozzarella cheese, chopped
- salt and pepper

1 Preheat the oven to 200°C/400°F/Gas Mark 6. Grease a rectangular ovenproof dish.

2 Melt the butter in a saucepan over a low heat. Add the flour and mustard powder and stir until smooth. Simmer gently for 2 minutes, then gradually add the milk, whisking until smooth. Bring to the boil, reduce the heat and simmer for 2 minutes. Remove from the heat and reserve. Cover the surface of the sauce with clingfilm to prevent a skin from forming.

3 Heat the oil in a frying pan. Add the onion and garlic and cook gently for 5 minutes, or until softened. Add the mushrooms and cook for 5 minutes, or until softened. Stir in the wine and boil rapidly until almost evaporated, then stir in the tomatoes. Bring to the boil, reduce the heat and simmer, covered, for 15 minutes. Season to taste with salt and pepper and set aside.

4 Spoon half the tomato mixture over the base of the prepared dish, top with half the fish and scallops and layer half the lasagne over the top. Pour over half the white sauce and sprinkle over half the mozzarella. Repeat these layers, finishing with sauce and mozzarella.

5 Bake in the preheated oven for 35–40 minutes, or until golden and the fish is cooked through. Remove from the oven and leave to stand for 10 minutes before serving.

layered salmon & prawn spaghetti

serves 6
- 350 g/12 oz dried spaghetti
- 70 g/2½ oz butter, plus extra for greasing
- 200 g/7 oz smoked salmon, cut into strips
- 280 g/10 oz large cooked peeled prawns
- 300 ml/10 fl oz béchamel sauce (see page 9)
- 115 g/4 oz freshly grated Parmesan cheese
- salt
- rocket leaves, to garnish

1 Preheat the oven to 180°C/350°F/Gas Mark 4. Grease a large ovenproof dish.

2 Bring a large saucepan of lightly salted water to the boil. Add the pasta, return to the boil and cook for 8–10 minutes, until tender but still firm to the bite. Drain well, return to the saucepan, add 55 g/2 oz of the butter and toss well.

3 Spoon half the spaghetti into the prepared dish, cover with the smoked salmon, then top with the prawns. Pour over half the béchamel sauce and sprinkle with half the Parmesan. Add the remaining spaghetti, cover with the remaining sauce and sprinkle with the remaining Parmesan. Dice the remaining butter and dot it over the surface.

4 Bake in the preheated oven for 15 minutes, until the top is golden. Serve immediately, garnished with rocket leaves.

tuna pasta bake

serves 4–6

- 200 g/7 oz dried tagliatelle
- 25 g/1 oz butter
- 55 g/2 oz fresh breadcrumbs
- 400 ml/14 fl oz canned condensed cream of mushroom soup
- 125 ml/4 fl oz milk
- 2 celery sticks, chopped
- 1 red pepper, deseeded and chopped
- 1 green pepper, deseeded and chopped
- 140 g/5 oz mature Cheddar cheese, coarsely grated
- 2 tbsp chopped fresh parsley
- 200 g/7 oz canned tuna in oil, drained and flaked
- salt and pepper

1 Preheat the oven to 200°C/400°F/Gas Mark 6.

2 Bring a large saucepan of lightly salted water to the boil. Add the pasta, return to the boil and cook for 2 minutes fewer than specified on the packet instructions. Drain well and set aside.

3 Meanwhile, melt the butter in a separate small saucepan. Stir in the breadcrumbs, then remove from the heat and set aside.

4 Pour the soup into a saucepan over a medium heat, then stir in the milk, celery, peppers, half the cheese and the parsley. Add the tuna and stir in gently. Season to taste with salt and pepper. Heat just until small bubbles appear around the edge of the mixture – do not boil.

5 Stir the pasta into the saucepan and use 2 forks to mix all the ingredients together. Spoon the mixture into an ovenproof dish and spread it out.

6 Stir the remaining cheese into the breadcrumb mixture, then sprinkle over the top of the pasta mixture. Bake in the preheated oven for 20–25 minutes, until the topping is golden. Remove from the oven, then leave to stand for 5 minutes before serving.

Mmmm...
vegetables
& pulses

vegetable cassoulet

serves 8

- 650 g/1 lb 7 oz dried haricot beans, soaked overnight and drained
- 2 bay leaves
- 3 onions
- 4 cloves
- 1 tbsp olive oil
- 4 garlic cloves, finely chopped
- 4 leeks, sliced
- 800 g/1 lb 12 oz baby carrots
- 225 g/8 oz button mushrooms
- 800 g/1 lb 12 oz canned chopped tomatoes
- 4 tbsp chopped fresh parsley
- 1 tbsp chopped fresh savory
- 115 g/4 oz fresh breadcrumbs
- salt and pepper

1 Put the beans and bay leaves into a saucepan. Stud 1 of the onions with the cloves and add to the pan. Pour in enough water to cover and bring to the boil. Reduce the heat, cover and simmer for 1 hour, then drain, reserving the cooking liquid. Remove and discard the bay leaves and onion.

2 Preheat the oven to 180°C/350°F/Gas Mark 4.

3 Chop the remaining onions. Heat the oil in a flameproof casserole, then add the chopped onions, garlic and leeks and cook over a low heat, stirring occasionally, for 5 minutes, until softened.

4 Add the carrots, mushrooms and tomatoes, pour in 850 ml/1½ pints of the reserved cooking liquid and season to taste with salt and pepper. Bring to the boil, then reduce the heat, cover and simmer for 15 minutes.

5 Stir in the beans, parsley and savory and adjust the seasoning, adding salt and pepper if needed. Sprinkle with the breadcrumbs and transfer the casserole to the preheated oven. Bake, uncovered, for 40–45 minutes, until the topping is golden brown. Serve immediately.

ratatouille

serves 8
- 1 red pepper, quartered
- 1 orange pepper, quartered
- 1 green pepper, quartered
- 550 g / 1 lb 4 oz aubergines, thickly sliced
- 2 tbsp olive oil, plus extra for brushing
- 2 large onions, sliced
- 3 garlic cloves, finely chopped
- 450 g / 1 lb courgettes, thickly sliced
- 850 g / 1 lb 14 oz tomatoes, peeled, deseeded and chopped
- 1½ tsp herbes de Provence
- 2 bay leaves
- salt and pepper
- crusty bread, to serve

1 Preheat the grill. Put the pepper quarters, skin-side up, on a baking tray and grill until charred and blistered. Remove with tongs, put them into a polythene bag, tie the top and leave to cool. Meanwhile, spread out the aubergine slices on the baking tray, brush with oil and grill for 5 minutes, until lightly browned. Turn, brush with oil and grill for a further 5 minutes, until lightly browned. Remove with tongs.

2 Remove the peppers from the bag and peel off the skins. Remove and discard the seeds and membranes and cut the flesh into strips. Dice the aubergine slices.

3 Heat the oil in a large saucepan or flameproof casserole. Add the onions and cook over a low heat, stirring occasionally, for 8–10 minutes, until lightly browned. Add the garlic and courgettes and cook, stirring occasionally, for a further 10 minutes.

4 Stir in the peppers, aubergines, tomatoes, herbes de Provence and bay leaves. Season to taste with salt and pepper, then cover and simmer over a very low heat, stirring occasionally, for 25 minutes. Remove the lid and simmer, stirring occasionally, for a further 25–35 minutes, until the vegetables are tender.

5 Remove and discard the bay leaves. Serve the ratatouille immediately, if serving hot, or leave to cool, if serving at room temperature, accompanied by crusty bread.

vegetable chilli

serves 4

- 1 aubergine, cut into 2.5-cm/1-inch slices
- 1 tbsp olive oil, plus extra for brushing
- 1 large red or yellow onion, finely chopped
- 2 red or yellow peppers, deseeded and finely chopped
- 3–4 garlic cloves, finely chopped or crushed
- 800 g/1 lb 12 oz canned chopped tomatoes
- 1 tbsp mild chilli powder
- ½ tsp ground cumin
- ½ tsp dried oregano
- 2 small courgettes, quartered lengthways and sliced
- 400 g/14 oz canned kidney beans, drained and rinsed
- 450 ml/16 fl oz water
- 1 tbsp tomato purée
- 6 spring onions, finely chopped
- 115 g/4 oz Cheddar cheese, grated
- salt and pepper
- crusty bread, to serve

1 Brush the aubergine slices on one side with oil. Heat half the oil in a large heavy-based frying pan. Add the aubergine slices, oiled-side up, and cook over a medium heat for 5–6 minutes, or until browned on one side. Turn the slices over, cook on the other side until browned and transfer to a plate. Cut into bite-sized pieces and set aside.

2 Heat the remaining oil in a large saucepan over a medium heat. Add the onion and peppers and cook, stirring occasionally, for 3–4 minutes, or until the onion is just softened but not browned. Add the garlic and cook for a further 2–3 minutes, or until the onion just begins to colour.

3 Add the tomatoes, chilli powder, cumin and oregano. Season to taste with salt and pepper. Bring just to the boil, reduce the heat, cover and simmer gently for 15 minutes.

4 Add the courgettes, aubergine pieces and kidney beans. Stir in the water and tomato purée. Return to the boil, then cover the saucepan and simmer for a further 45 minutes, or until the vegetables are tender. Taste and adjust the seasoning, adding salt and pepper if needed.

5 Ladle into warmed bowls and top with the spring onions and cheese. Serve immediately with crusty bread.

tuscan bean stew

serves 4

- 1 large fennel bulb
- 2 tbsp olive oil
- 1 red onion, cut into small wedges
- 2–4 garlic cloves, sliced
- 1 fresh green chilli, deseeded and chopped
- 1 small aubergine, about 225 g/8 oz, cut into chunks
- 2 tbsp tomato purée
- 450–600 ml/16 fl oz–1 pint vegetable stock
- 450 g/1 lb ripe tomatoes
- 1 tbsp balsamic vinegar
- a few fresh oregano sprigs
- 400 g/14 oz canned borlotti beans
- 400 g/14 oz canned flageolet beans
- 1 yellow pepper, deseeded and cut into small strips
- 1 courgette, sliced into half moons
- 55 g/2 oz stoned black olives
- salt and pepper
- 25 g/1 oz Parmesan cheese shavings
- crusty bread, to serve

1 Trim the fennel and reserve any feathery fronds, then cut the bulb into small strips. Heat the oil in a large heavy-based saucepan with a tight-fitting lid and cook the onion, garlic, chilli and fennel strips, stirring frequently, for 5–8 minutes, or until softened.

2 Add the aubergine and cook, stirring frequently, for 5 minutes. Blend the tomato purée with a little of the stock in a jug and pour into the pan, then add the remaining stock, the tomatoes, vinegar and oregano. Bring to the boil, then reduce the heat, cover and simmer for 15 minutes, or until the tomatoes have begun to collapse.

3 Drain and rinse the beans, then drain again. Add them to the pan with the yellow pepper, courgette and olives. Simmer for a further 15 minutes, or until all the vegetables are tender. Taste and adjust the seasoning, adding salt and pepper if needed. Scatter with the Parmesan shavings and serve immediately, garnished with the reserved fennel fronds and accompanied by crusty bread.

italian vegetable stew

serves 4

- 4 garlic cloves
- 1 small acorn squash, peeled and deseeded
- 1 red onion, sliced
- 2 leeks, sliced
- 1 aubergine, sliced
- 1 small celeriac, diced
- 2 turnips, sliced
- 2 plum tomatoes, chopped
- 1 carrot, sliced
- 1 courgette, sliced
- 2 red peppers, deseeded and sliced
- 1 fennel bulb, sliced
- 175 g/6 oz chard
- 2 bay leaves
- ½ tsp fennel seeds
- ½ tsp chilli powder
- pinch of each dried thyme, dried oregano and sugar
- 25 g/1 oz fresh basil leaves, torn
- 125 ml/4 fl oz extra virgin olive oil
- 225 ml/8 fl oz vegetable stock
- 4 tbsp chopped fresh parsley
- salt and pepper
- 2 tbsp freshly grated Parmesan cheese, to serve

1 Finely chop the garlic and dice the squash. Put them in a large heavy-based saucepan with all the other vegetables, the bay leaves, fennel seeds, chilli powder, thyme, oregano, sugar and half the basil. Pour in the oil and stock. Mix together well, then bring to the boil.

2 Reduce the heat, cover and simmer for 30 minutes, or until all the vegetables are tender.

3 Sprinkle in the remaining basil and the parsley and season to taste with salt and pepper. Serve immediately, sprinkled with the Parmesan.

lentil bolognese

serves 4
- 1 tsp vegetable oil
- 1 tsp crushed garlic
- 25 g/1 oz onion, finely chopped
- 25 g/1 oz leek, finely chopped
- 25 g/1 oz celery, finely chopped
- 25 g/1 oz green pepper, deseeded and finely chopped
- 25 g/1 oz carrot, finely chopped
- 25 g/1 oz courgette, finely chopped
- 85 g/3 oz flat mushrooms, diced
- 4 tbsp red wine
- pinch of dried thyme
- 400 g/14 oz canned chopped tomatoes, strained through a colander, juice and pulp reserved separately
- 4 tbsp dried Puy or green lentils, cooked
- 2 tsp lemon juice
- 1 tsp sugar
- 3 tbsp chopped fresh basil, plus extra to garnish
- salt and pepper
- cooked spaghetti, to serve

1 Place a large saucepan over a low heat, add the oil and garlic and cook, stirring, until golden brown. Add all the vegetables, except the mushrooms, increase the heat to medium and cook, stirring occasionally, for 10–12 minutes, or until softened and there is no liquid from the vegetables left in the pan.

2 Add the mushrooms and increase the heat to high. Add the wine and cook for 2 minutes, then stir in the thyme and the juice from the tomatoes and cook until reduced by half.

3 Add the lentils, stir in the tomato pulp and cook for a further 3–4 minutes. Remove the pan from the heat and stir in the lemon juice, sugar and basil. Season to taste with salt and pepper.

4 Serve the sauce immediately with spaghetti, garnished with basil.

vegetable & lentil casserole

serves 4

- 10 cloves
- 1 onion, peeled but kept whole
- 225 g/8 oz Puy or green lentils
- 1 bay leaf
- 1.5 litres/2¾ pints vegetable stock
- 2 leeks, sliced
- 2 potatoes, diced
- 2 carrots, chopped
- 3 courgettes, sliced
- 1 celery stick, chopped
- 1 red pepper, deseeded and chopped
- 1 tbsp lemon juice
- salt and pepper

1 Preheat the oven to 180°C/350°F/Gas Mark 4.

2 Press the cloves into the onion. Put the lentils into a large casserole, add the onion and bay leaf and pour in the stock. Cover and cook in the preheated oven for 1 hour.

3 Remove the onion and discard the cloves. Slice the onion and return it to the casserole with all the vegetables. Stir thoroughly and season to taste with salt and pepper. Cover and return to the oven for 1 hour.

4 Discard the bay leaf. Stir in the lemon juice and serve immediately straight from the casserole.

vegetable curry

serves 4

- 1 aubergine
- 225 g/8 oz turnips
- 350 g/12 oz new potatoes
- 225 g/8 oz cauliflower
- 225 g/8 oz button mushrooms
- 1 large onion
- 3 carrots
- 6 tbsp ghee
- 2 garlic cloves, crushed
- 4 tsp finely chopped fresh ginger
- 1–2 fresh green chillies, deseeded and chopped
- 1 tbsp paprika
- 2 tsp ground coriander
- 1 tbsp mild or medium curry powder
- 450 ml/16 fl oz vegetable stock
- 400 g/14 oz canned chopped tomatoes
- 1 green pepper, deseeded and sliced
- 1 tbsp cornflour
- 150 ml/5 fl oz coconut milk
- 2–3 tbsp ground almonds
- salt
- fresh coriander sprigs, to garnish
- cooked rice, to serve

1 Cut the aubergine, turnips and potatoes into 1-cm/½-inch cubes. Divide the cauliflower into small florets. Leave the button mushrooms whole or slice them thickly, if preferred. Slice the onion and carrots.

2 Heat the ghee in a large heavy-based saucepan. Add the onion, turnips, potatoes and cauliflower and cook over a low heat, stirring frequently, for 3 minutes. Add the garlic, ginger, chilli, paprika, ground coriander and curry powder and cook, stirring, for 1 minute.

3 Add the stock, tomatoes, aubergine and mushrooms, and season to taste with salt. Cover and simmer, stirring occasionally, for 30 minutes, or until the vegetables are tender. Add the green pepper and carrots, cover and cook for a further 5 minutes.

4 Place the cornflour and coconut milk in a bowl, mix to form a smooth paste and stir into the vegetable mixture. Add the ground almonds and simmer, stirring constantly, for 2 minutes. Taste and adjust the seasoning, adding salt if needed. Transfer to warmed serving plates, garnish with coriander sprigs and serve immediately with rice.

spicy chickpea casserole

serves 6

- 1 tbsp cumin seeds
- 2 tbsp coriander seeds
- 2 tsp dried oregano or thyme
- 5 tbsp vegetable oil
- 2 onions, chopped
- 1 red pepper, deseeded and cut into 2-cm/¾-inch chunks
- 1 aubergine, cut into 2-cm/¾-inch chunks
- 2 garlic cloves, chopped
- 1 fresh green chilli, deseeded and chopped
- 400 g/14 oz canned chopped tomatoes
- 400 g/14 oz canned chickpeas, drained and rinsed
- 225 g/8 oz green beans, cut into 2-cm/¾-inch lengths
- 600 ml/1 pint vegetable stock
- 3 tbsp chopped fresh coriander, plus extra leaves to garnish

1 Dry-fry the seeds in a heavy-based frying pan for a few seconds, until aromatic. Add the oregano and cook for a further few seconds. Remove from the heat, transfer to a mortar and crush with a pestle.

2 Heat the oil in a large flameproof casserole. Cook the onions, red pepper and aubergine for 10 minutes, until soft. Add the ground seed mixture, the garlic and chilli and cook for a further 2 minutes.

3 Add the tomatoes, chickpeas, green beans and stock. Bring to the boil, cover and simmer gently for 1 hour, then stir in the chopped coriander. Serve immediately, garnished with coriander leaves.

Mmmm...

vegetable goulash

serves 4

- 15 g/½ oz sun-dried tomatoes (not in oil), chopped
- 225 g/8 oz Puy lentils
- 600 ml/1 pint water
- 2 tbsp olive oil
- ½–1 tsp crushed dried chillies
- 2–3 garlic cloves, chopped
- 1 large onion, cut into small wedges
- 1 small celeriac, cut into small chunks
- 225 g/8 oz carrots, sliced
- 225 g/8 oz new potatoes, scrubbed and cut into chunks
- 1 small acorn squash, deseeded, peeled and cut into small chunks, about 225 g/8 oz prepared weight
- 2 tbsp tomato purée
- 300 ml/10 fl oz vegetable stock
- 1–2 tsp hot paprika
- a few fresh thyme sprigs, plus extra to garnish
- 450 g/1 lb ripe tomatoes
- soured cream and crusty bread, to serve

1 Put the sun-dried tomatoes in a small heatproof bowl, cover with almost-boiling water and leave to soak for 15–20 minutes. Drain, reserving the soaking liquid.

2 Meanwhile, rinse and drain the lentils, then put them in a saucepan with the water and bring to the boil. Reduce the heat, cover and simmer for 15 minutes. Drain and set aside.

3 Heat the oil in a large heavy-based saucepan with a tight-fitting lid and cook the chillies, garlic and vegetables, stirring frequently, for 5–8 minutes, until softened. Blend the tomato purée with a little of the stock in a jug and pour over the vegetable mixture, then add the remaining stock, the lentils, the sun-dried tomatoes and their soaking liquid, and the paprika and thyme sprigs.

4 Bring to the boil, then reduce the heat, cover and simmer for 15 minutes. Add the fresh tomatoes and simmer for a further 15 minutes, or until the vegetables and lentils are tender. Transfer to warmed serving bowls, top with spoonfuls of soured cream and garnish with thyme sprigs. Serve immediately with crusty bread.

cold weather vegetable casserole

serves 4
- 50 g/1¾ oz butter
- 2 leeks, sliced
- 2 carrots, sliced
- 2 potatoes, cut into bite-sized pieces
- 1 swede, cut into bite-sized pieces
- 2 courgettes, sliced
- 1 fennel bulb, halved and sliced
- 2 tbsp plain flour
- 425 g/15 oz canned butter beans
- 450 ml/16 fl oz vegetable stock
- 2 tbsp tomato purée
- 1 tsp dried thyme
- 2 bay leaves
- salt and pepper

dumplings
- 115 g/4 oz self-raising flour
- pinch of salt
- 55 g/2 oz vegetable suet
- 2 tbsp chopped fresh parsley
- 4 tbsp water

1 Melt the butter in a large frying pan over a low heat. Add the leeks, carrots, potatoes, swede, courgettes and fennel and cook, stirring occasionally, for 10 minutes. Stir in the flour and cook, stirring constantly for 1 minute. Stir in the can juices from the beans, the stock, tomato purée, thyme and bay leaves. Season to taste with salt and pepper. Bring to the boil, stirring constantly, then cover and simmer for 10 minutes.

2 To make the dumplings sift the flour and salt into a mixing bowl, add the suet and mix well. Stir in the parsley and then pour in enough of the water to form a firm but soft dough. Break the dough into 8 pieces and roll them into round dumplings.

3 Add the butter beans and the dumplings to the pan, pushing them down under the liquid. Cover and simmer for a further 30 minutes, or until the dumplings have doubled in size.

4 Remove and discard the bay leaves and serve the stew and dumplings immediately.

lentil & rice casserole

serves 4

- 225 g/8 oz red lentils
- 55 g/2 oz long-grain rice
- 1.2 litres/2 pints vegetable stock
- 1 leek, cut into chunks
- 3 garlic cloves, crushed
- 400 g/14 oz canned chopped tomatoes
- 1 tsp ground cumin
- 1 tsp chilli powder
- 1 tsp garam masala
- 1 red pepper, deseeded and sliced
- 100 g/3½ oz small broccoli florets
- 8 baby corn, halved lengthways
- 55 g/2 oz French beans, halved
- 1 tbsp shredded fresh basil, plus extra sprigs to garnish
- salt and pepper

1 Place the lentils, rice and stock in a large flameproof casserole and cook over a low heat, stirring occasionally, for 20 minutes.

2 Add the leek, garlic, tomatoes, cumin, chilli powder, garam masala, red pepper, broccoli, baby corn and French beans to the casserole.

3 Bring to the boil, then reduce the heat, cover and simmer for 10–15 minutes, or until the vegetables are tender.

4 Add the shredded basil and season to taste with salt and pepper.

5 Garnish with basil sprigs and serve immediately.

root vegetable & pumpkin casserole

serves 4–6

- 1 onion, sliced
- 2 leeks, sliced
- 2 celery sticks, chopped
- 2 carrots, thinly sliced
- 1 red pepper, deseeded and sliced
- 225 g/8 oz pumpkin flesh (prepared weight), diced
- 450 g/1 lb mixed root vegetables, such as sweet potato, parsnip and swede (prepared weight), diced
- 400 g/14 oz canned chopped tomatoes
- 150–200 ml/5–7 fl oz dry cider
- 2 tsp herbes de Provence
- salt and pepper
- fresh flat-leaf parsley leaves, to garnish

1 Preheat the oven to 180°C/350°F/Gas Mark 4.

2 Place the onion, leeks, celery, carrots, red pepper, pumpkin and root vegetables in a large casserole and mix well. Stir in the tomatoes, 150 ml/5 fl oz of the cider and the herbes de Provence. Season to taste with salt and pepper.

3 Cover and bake in the preheated oven, stirring once or twice and adding a little extra cider if needed, for 1¼–1½ hours, or until the vegetables are cooked through and tender. Serve immediately, garnished with parsley leaves.

spring stew

serves 4

- 225 g/8 oz dried haricot beans, soaked overnight and drained
- 2 tbsp olive oil
- 4–8 baby onions, halved
- 2 celery sticks, cut into 5-mm/¼-inch slices
- 225 g/8 oz baby carrots, scrubbed and halved if large
- 300 g/10½ oz new potatoes, scrubbed and halved or quartered if large
- 850 ml-1.2 litres/1½–2 pints vegetable stock
- bouquet garni
- 1½–2 tbsp light soy sauce
- 85 g/3 oz baby corn
- 115 g/4 oz shelled broad beans, thawed if frozen
- ½–1 Savoy or spring cabbage, about 225 g/8 oz
- 1½ tbsp cornflour
- 2 tbsp cold water
- salt and pepper
- 55–85 g/2–3 oz Parmesan or mature Cheddar cheese, grated, to serve

1 Put the beans in a large pan, add water to cover and bring to the boil. Boil the beans rapidly for 20 minutes, then drain and set aside.

2 Heat the oil in a large heavy-based saucepan with a tight-fitting lid, add the onions, celery, carrots and potatoes, and cook, stirring frequently, for 5 minutes, or until softened. Add the stock, drained beans, bouquet garni and soy sauce, then bring to the boil. Reduce the heat, cover and simmer for 12 minutes.

3 Add the baby corn and broad beans and season to taste with salt and pepper. Simmer for a further 3 minutes.

4 Meanwhile, discard the outer leaves and hard central core from the cabbage and shred the leaves. Add to the saucepan and simmer for a further 3–5 minutes, or until all the vegetables are tender.

5 Blend the cornflour with the water, stir into the saucepan and cook, stirring, for 4–6 minutes, or until the liquid has thickened. Spoon into serving bowls and sprinkle over the cheese. Serve immediately.

bean & pasta bake

serves 4
- 225 g/8 oz dried haricot beans, soaked overnight and drained
- 225 g/8 oz dried penne
- 6 tbsp olive oil
- 850 ml/1½ pints vegetable stock
- 2 large onions, sliced
- 2 garlic cloves, chopped
- 2 bay leaves
- 1 tsp dried oregano
- 1 tsp dried thyme
- 5 tbsp red wine
- 2 tbsp tomato purée
- 2 celery sticks, sliced
- 1 fennel bulb, sliced
- 115 g/4 oz mushrooms, sliced
- 225 g/8 oz tomatoes, sliced
- 1 tsp dark muscovado sugar
- 55 g/2 oz dry white breadcrumbs
- salt and pepper
- crusty bread, to serve

1 Preheat the oven to 180°C/350°F/Gas Mark 4.

2 Put the beans in a large pan, add water to cover and bring to the boil. Boil the beans rapidly for 20 minutes, then drain and set aside.

3 Cook the pasta in a large saucepan of boiling salted water, adding 1 tablespoon of the oil, for 3 minutes. Drain and set aside.

4 Put the beans in a large flameproof casserole and pour in the stock, then stir in the remaining oil, the onions, garlic, bay leaves, herbs, wine and tomato purée. Bring to the boil, cover and cook in the preheated oven for 2 hours.

5 Remove the casserole from the oven and add the reserved pasta, the celery, fennel, mushrooms and tomatoes and season to taste with salt and pepper. Stir in the sugar and sprinkle the breadcrumbs on top. Cover, return to the oven and continue cooking for 1 hour. Serve immediately with crusty bread.

mixed bean & vegetable crumble

serves 4
- 1 large onion, chopped
- 125 g/4½ oz canned red kidney beans (drained weight)
- 125 g/4½ oz canned butter beans (drained weight)
- 125 g/4½ oz canned chickpeas (drained weight)
- 2 courgettes, roughly chopped
- 2 large carrots, roughly chopped
- 4 tomatoes, peeled and roughly chopped
- 2 celery sticks, chopped
- 300 ml/10 fl oz vegetable stock
- 2 tbsp tomato purée
- salt and pepper

crumble topping
- 85 g/3 oz wholemeal breadcrumbs
- 25 g/1 oz hazelnuts, very finely chopped
- 1 heaped tbsp chopped fresh parsley
- 115 g/4 oz Cheddar cheese, grated

1 Preheat the oven to 180°C/350°F/Gas Mark 4.

2 Put the onion, kidney beans, butter beans, chickpeas, courgettes, carrots, tomatoes and celery in a large ovenproof dish. Mix together the stock and tomato purée and pour over the vegetables. Season to taste with salt and pepper. Transfer to the preheated oven and bake for 15 minutes.

3 Meanwhile, to make the crumble topping, put the breadcrumbs in a large bowl, add the hazelnuts, parsley and cheese and mix together well.

4 Remove the vegetables from the oven and carefully sprinkle over the crumble topping. Do not press down or it will sink into the vegetables and go mushy.

5 Return the crumble to the oven and bake for 30 minutes, or until the crumble topping is golden brown. Remove from the oven and serve immediately.

206

spicy vegetable cobbler

serves 4

- 1 large onion, sliced
- 2 courgettes, sliced
- 85 g/3 oz mushrooms, sliced
- 2 large carrots, roughly chopped
- 225 g/8 oz canned black-eyed beans (drained weight)
- 175 g/6 oz canned haricot beans (drained weight)
- 400 g/14 oz canned chopped tomatoes
- 1 tsp mild chilli powder
- salt and pepper

cobbler topping

- 175 g/6 oz self-raising flour, plus extra for dusting
- 2 tsp baking powder
- ½ tsp paprika
- pinch of salt
- 40 g/1½ oz unsalted butter
- 4–5 tbsp milk

1 Preheat the oven to 200°C/400°F/Gas Mark 6.

2 Put the onion, courgettes, mushrooms, carrots, black-eyed beans, haricot beans and tomatoes in a casserole. Sprinkle over the chilli powder and season to taste with salt and pepper. Transfer to the preheated oven and bake for 15 minutes.

3 Meanwhile, to make the cobbler topping, sift the flour, baking powder, paprika and salt into a large mixing bowl. Rub in the butter until the mixture resembles fine breadcrumbs, then stir in enough of the milk to make a smooth dough. Transfer to a lightly floured work surface, knead lightly, then roll out to a thickness of about 1 cm/½ inch. Cut out rounds using a 5-cm/2-inch biscuit cutter.

4 Remove the casserole from the oven and arrange the dough rounds over the top, then return to the oven and bake for 30 minutes, or until the cobbler topping has risen and is lightly golden. Serve immediately.

spinach & butternut squash bake

serves 2

- 250 g/9 oz butternut squash (peeled weight), deseeded and cut into bite-sized cubes
- 2 small red onions, each cut into 8 wedges
- 2 tsp vegetable oil
- 125 g/4¼ oz baby spinach leaves
- 1 tbsp water
- 2 tbsp wholemeal breadcrumbs
- pepper

white sauce

- 250 ml/9 fl oz skimmed milk
- 20 g/¾ oz cornflour
- 1 tsp mustard powder
- 1 small onion
- 2 bay leaves
- 4 tsp grated Parmesan or pecorino cheese

1 Preheat the oven to 200°C/400°F/Gas Mark 6 and warm an ovenproof serving dish.

2 Arrange the squash and red onions on a baking tray and coat with the oil and plenty of pepper. Bake in the preheated oven for 20 minutes, turning once.

3 To make the sauce, put the milk into a small saucepan with the cornflour, mustard powder, onion and bay leaves. Whisk over a medium heat until thick. Remove from the heat, discard the onion and bay leaves and stir in the cheese. Set aside, stirring occasionally to prevent a skin from forming.

4 When the squash is nearly cooked, put the spinach in a large saucepan with the water and stir over a medium heat for 2–3 minutes, or until just wilted.

5 Put half the squash mixture in the warmed ovenproof dish and top with half the spinach. Repeat the layers. Pour over the white sauce and sprinkle over the breadcrumbs.

6 Transfer to the oven and bake for 15–20 minutes, until the topping is golden and bubbling. Serve immediately.

baked beans with sweetcorn topping

serves 4–6

- 6 tbsp olive oil or butter
- 750 g/1 lb 10 oz onions, finely sliced
- 3–4 garlic cloves, finely chopped
- 1 tsp cumin seeds
- 1 tsp fresh or dried oregano
- 500 g/1 lb 2 oz fresh tomatoes, peeled and chopped, or canned chopped tomatoes
- 500 g/1 lb 2 oz pumpkin, peeled, deseeded and cut into small dice
- 750 g/1 lb 10 oz cooked pinto or borlotti beans, drained and rinsed
- 2 tbsp green olives, stoned and chopped
- 2 tbsp raisins
- 1 tbsp icing sugar
- 1 tsp dried chilli flakes
- salt and pepper

topping

- 1.3 kg/3 lb fresh or frozen sweetcorn
- 375 ml/13 fl oz full-fat milk
- 1 egg, beaten
- salt and pepper

1 Preheat the oven to 180°C/350°F/Gas Mark 4.

2 Heat 4 tablespoons of the oil in a heavy-based saucepan, add the onions and garlic and cook over a very low heat, stirring occasionally, for 20–30 minutes, or until softened. Add the cumin seeds, oregano and tomatoes and simmer for 10 minutes, or until you have a thick sauce.

3 Add the pumpkin and heat until bubbling. Reduce the heat to low, cover and cook for a further 10–15 minutes, or until the pumpkin is softened but not collapsed. Stir in the beans, olives and raisins. Reheat gently and simmer for 5 minutes. Season to taste with salt and pepper.

4 Put the sweetcorn in a blender or food processor with the milk and blend to a purée. Transfer to a saucepan and cook, stirring constantly, for 5 minutes, or until the mixture has thickened slightly. Remove from the heat and leave to cool. Stir in the egg and season to taste with salt and pepper.

5 Spread the bean mixture in an ovenproof dish and top with a thick layer of the sweetcorn mixture. Drizzle with the remaining oil and sprinkle with the sugar and chilli flakes. Bake in the preheated oven for 30 minutes, or until browned and bubbling. Serve immediately.

baked aubergines

serves 4
- 4 aubergines
- 3 tbsp olive oil, plus extra for oiling
- 300 g/10½ oz mozzarella cheese, thinly sliced
- 4 slices Parma ham, shredded
- 1 tbsp chopped fresh marjoram
- 25 g/1 oz Parmesan cheese, grated
- salt and pepper

tomato sauce
- 4 tbsp olive oil
- 1 large onion, sliced
- 4 garlic cloves, crushed
- 400 g/14 oz canned chopped tomatoes
- 450 g/1 lb fresh tomatoes, peeled and chopped
- 4 tbsp chopped fresh parsley
- 600 ml/1 pint hot vegetable stock
- 1 tbsp sugar
- 2 tbsp lemon juice
- 150 ml/5 fl oz dry white wine
- salt and pepper

white sauce
- 25 g/1 oz butter
- 25 g/1 oz plain flour
- 1 tsp mustard powder
- 300 ml/10 fl oz milk
- freshly grated nutmeg
- salt and pepper

1 Preheat the oven to 190°C/375°F/Gas Mark 5. Lightly oil a large ovenproof dish.

2 To make the tomato sauce, heat the oil in a large frying pan. Add the onion and garlic and fry until just beginning to soften. Add the canned and fresh tomatoes, parsley, stock, sugar and lemon juice. Cover and simmer for 15 minutes. Stir in the wine and season to taste with salt and pepper.

3 Thinly slice the aubergines lengthways. Bring a large saucepan of water to the boil and cook the aubergine slices for 5 minutes. Drain on kitchen paper.

4 Pour half the tomato sauce into the prepared dish with half the aubergines and drizzle with the oil. Cover with half the mozzarella, Parma ham and marjoram. Season to taste with salt and pepper. Repeat the layers.

5 To make the white sauce, melt the butter in a large saucepan, then add the flour and mustard powder. Stir until smooth and cook over a low heat for 2 minutes. Slowly beat in the milk. Simmer gently for 2 minutes. Remove from the heat, then season to taste with nutmeg, salt and pepper.

6 Spoon the white sauce over the aubergine and tomato mixture, then sprinkle with the Parmesan. Bake in the preheated oven for 35–40 minutes, until the topping is golden. Serve immediately.

vegetable lasagne

serves 4

- 1 aubergine, sliced
- 3 tbsp olive oil
- 2 garlic cloves, crushed
- 1 red onion,
  halved and sliced
- 3 mixed peppers,
  deseeded and diced
- 225 g/8 oz mixed
  mushrooms, sliced
- 2 celery sticks, sliced
- 1 courgette, diced
- ½ tsp chilli powder
- ½ tsp ground cumin
- 2 tomatoes, chopped
- 300 ml/10 fl oz passata
- 2 tbsp chopped fresh basil
- 8 no pre-cook lasagne
  verde sheets
- salt and pepper

cheese sauce

- 25 g/1 oz butter
  or margarine
- 1 tbsp plain flour
- 150 ml/5 fl oz vegetable
  stock
- 300 ml/10 fl oz milk
- 75 g/2¾ oz Cheddar
  cheese, grated
- 1 tsp Dijon mustard
- 1 tbsp chopped fresh basil
- 1 egg, beaten

1 Place the aubergine slices in a colander, sprinkle with salt and leave for 20 minutes. Rinse under cold water, drain and reserve.

2 Preheat the oven to 180°C/350°F/Gas Mark 4.

3 Heat the oil in a saucepan. Add the garlic and onion and sauté for 1–2 minutes. Add the peppers, mushrooms, celery and courgette and cook, stirring constantly, for 3–4 minutes. Stir in the chilli powder and cumin and cook for 1 minute. Mix in the tomatoes, passata and basil and season to taste with salt and pepper.

4 For the cheese sauce, melt the butter in a saucepan. Stir in the flour and cook for 1 minute. Remove from the heat and gradually stir in the stock and milk. Return to the heat, then add half the cheese and all the mustard. Boil, stirring, until thickened. Stir in the basil. Remove from the heat and stir in the egg.

5 Place half the lasagne sheets in a rectangular ovenproof dish. Top with half the vegetable mixture and half the aubergine slices. Repeat the layers, then spoon the cheese sauce on top. Sprinkle with the remaining cheese and bake in the preheated oven for 40 minutes, or until golden and bubbling. Serve immediately.

vegetable cannelloni

serves 4

- 12 dried cannelloni tubes
- 125 ml/4 fl oz olive oil, plus extra for oiling
- 1 aubergine, diced
- 225 g/8 oz spinach
- 2 garlic cloves, crushed
- 1 tsp ground cumin
- 85 g/3 oz mushrooms, chopped
- 55 g/2 oz mozzarella cheese, sliced
- salt and pepper
- lamb's lettuce, to garnish

tomato sauce

- 1 tbsp olive oil
- 1 onion, chopped
- 2 garlic cloves, crushed
- 800 g/1 lb 12 oz canned chopped tomatoes
- 1 tsp caster sugar
- 2 tbsp chopped fresh basil

1 Preheat the oven to 190°C/375°F/Gas Mark 5. Lightly oil a large ovenproof dish.

2 Bring a large heavy-based saucepan of lightly salted water to the boil. Add the cannelloni tubes, return to the boil and cook for 8–10 minutes, or until tender but still firm to the bite. Drain on kitchen paper and pat dry.

3 Heat the oil in a frying pan over a medium heat. Add the aubergine and cook, stirring frequently, for about 2–3 minutes.

4 Add the spinach, garlic, cumin and mushrooms and reduce the heat. Season to taste with salt and pepper and cook, stirring, for about 2–3 minutes. Spoon the mixture into the cannelloni tubes and put into the prepared dish in a single layer.

5 To make the tomato sauce, heat the oil in a pan over a medium heat. Add the onion and garlic and cook for 1 minute. Add the tomatoes, sugar and basil and bring to the boil. Reduce the heat and simmer for about 5 minutes. Spoon the sauce over the cannelloni tubes.

6 Arrange the mozzarella over the top and bake in the preheated oven for about 30 minutes, or until the cheese is golden brown and bubbling. Serve immediately, garnished with lamb's lettuce.

oven-baked risotto with mushrooms

serves 4
- 4 tbsp olive oil
- 400 g/14 oz portobello or large field mushrooms, thickly sliced
- 115 g/4 oz pancetta or thick-cut smoked bacon, diced
- 1 large onion, finely chopped
- 2 garlic cloves, finely chopped
- 350 g/12 oz risotto rice
- 1.3 litres/2¼ pints simmering chicken or vegetable stock
- 2 tbsp chopped fresh tarragon or flat-leaf parsley
- 85 g/3 oz freshly grated Parmesan cheese, plus extra for sprinkling
- salt and pepper

1 Preheat the oven to 180°C/350°F/Gas Mark 4.

2 Heat half the oil in a large heavy-based frying pan over a high heat. Add the mushrooms and stir-fry for 2–3 minutes, until golden. Transfer to a plate. Add the pancetta to the frying pan and cook, stirring frequently, for 2 minutes, or until crisp and golden. Transfer to the plate with the mushrooms.

3 Heat the remaining oil in a large flameproof casserole over a medium heat. Add the onion and cook, stirring occasionally, for 2 minutes. Add the garlic and cook for 1 minute. Reduce the heat, add the rice and mix to coat in oil. Cook, stirring constantly, for 2–3 minutes, or until the grains are translucent.

4 Gradually stir the hot stock into the rice, then add the mushroom and pancetta mixture and the tarragon. Season to taste with salt and pepper. Bring to the boil.

5 Cover and bake in the preheated oven for 20 minutes, or until the rice is almost tender and most of the liquid is absorbed. Uncover and stir in the Parmesan. Bake for a further 15 minutes, until the rice is creamy. Serve immediately, sprinkled with extra Parmesan.

Index